Welcome back – After the holidays

1 Where were they? ▸ pp. 6–7

 a) Where were the Bristol kids in the holidays? Who says what? Match the pictures and the speech bubbles.

We had great holidays. I was in the pool or on the beach every day. I love Majorca.

Bristol is a great place in summer. We stayed at home because we had lots of nice guests at the B&B.

We were in a caravan by the sea. It was fun and we met a nice girl, a very nice girl.

Hello! Hello! I was at home with Jack, but we had some nice trips. Nice trips.

I had fantastic holidays. I went to New York! My cousin Jay lives there.

b) Now write sentences about the kids and Polly with was or were.

Jack was at home in Bristol.

Ananda

0101

2 WORDS Holiday words ▸ pp. 6–7

Write the missing words. ▸ What's the word in the yellow boxes?

1 Let's play football on the *beach* _____ !

2 Let's write a funny _____ to Grandma!

3 We were in a nice _____ by the sea.

4 We stayed at a hotel in the _____ .

5 The _____ from our window was fantastic.

6 The _____ was too cold, so we went swimming in the pool.

7 New York looked fantastic from the _____ .

8 Majorca is an _____ .

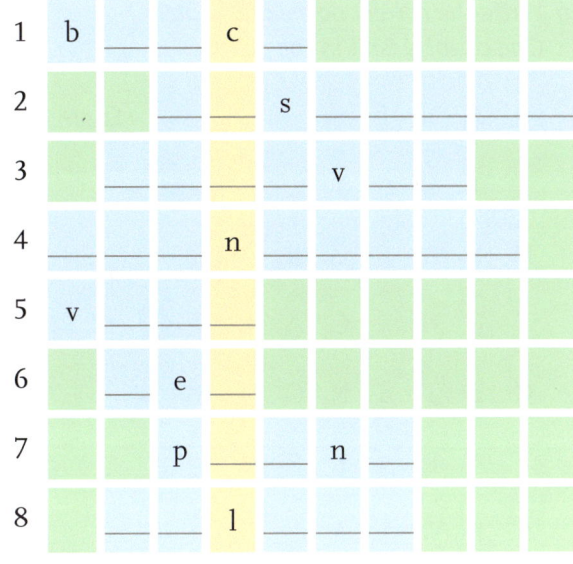

0102 ▸ It's a very nice place for a holiday: _____ .

*O = leichte Übung

○ **3 WORDS   What's the weather like?** ▸ *p. 8*

Choose two correct words and write sentences.

cold • *hot* • *sunny* • rainy

It's hot and sunny.

windy • cloudy • rainy • cold

rainy • sunny • stormy • hot

warm • sunny • cold • foggy

0203

Now you

Write three sentences about the weather.

Today the weather _____ .

I like it when _____ .

Yesterday it _____ .

4 Extra **WORDS   Countries** ▸ *p. 8 • p. 219*

a) *Write the correct name and match.*
    One country isn't in the picture.

P	A	N	I	S				*Spain*
T	I	L	A	Y				
N	F	A	E	C	R			
Y	R	N	E	G	A	M		
C	L	T	S	N	O	D	A	
T	A	R	A	L	S	U	I	A
S	E	W	L	A				

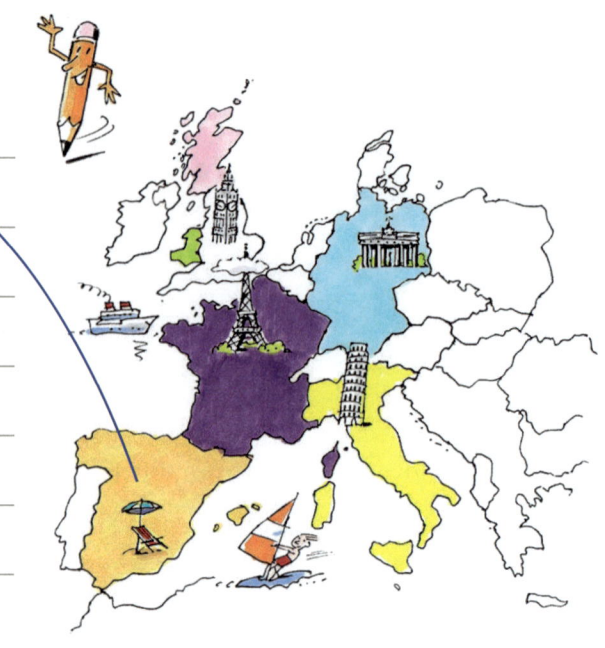

0204   *b)* *Which country isn't in the picture?* _____

5 WORDS Holiday talk ▶ *p. 9*

Becky, Lucy, Florian and some friends are talking about their holidays.
Look at their photos. Where were they? Complete the sentences.

at a hotel by the sea • in the country • in the mountains • by car • by a lake • on the beach

1 *Becky*   We had a great time. We were in Italy. We stayed *at a hotel by the sea* _____ .

2 *Lucy*   We were in Scotland. We went _____ . We were in a caravan _____ .
It was warm and sunny. We had lots of fun.

3 *Florian*   I was in Germany at my uncle's house. He lives _____ near Munich[1].

4 *Nick*   We went to Germany too. We stayed in a holiday flat _____ .

5 *Emma*   We were in Spain. It was hot, so we were _____ every day.

And where was I? I wasn't abroad. I wasn't in a big hotel and I wasn't in a nice caravan. I was at Aunt Mildred's house – with Aunt Mildred and her big, scary dog …

Rhyme time

Holidays are lots of fun,
You can swim in the sea,
You can play in the sun.
New places to see,
New things to do,
I love holidays,
What about you?

●** **Now you**

Look at the photos in exercise 5 again. Where do you like to stay? In the mountains, by the sea or in the country?
At a hotel, in a holiday flat or in a caravan? What's best and why? Write at least four sentences in your exercise book.

0305

1 Munich [mjuːnik] *München*

** ● = schwierige Übung

Unit 1 Back to school

1 WORDS Where are the school words? ▶ pp. 10–11

Find the mistakes. Cross out the wrong words in the lists and write them in the correct lists.

At school	
~~dishwasher~~	
board	_____
armchair	
timetable	_____
PE	
station	_____
bedroom	
essays	_____
Art Club	
museum	_____

At home	
pets	
bridge	*dishwasher*
classmates	
teacher	_____
parents	
kitchen	_____
bathroom	
sports centre	_____
doorbell	
church	_____

In my town or village	
wardrobe	
shops	_____
library	
fish bowl	_____
morning break	
houses	_____
exercises	
tower	_____
Geography	
	_____

0401

2 STUDY SKILLS Describing pictures ▶ pp. 10–11 • SF (p. 117)

Look at the postcard and complete the text on the next page.

0402
0403

Choose from:

| at the top | on the right | on the left | in the middle | in the foreground |

| at the bottom | in the background |

At the top _____ of the postcard it says '*Welcome…*'

_____ there's a boy with a comic. _____ there's a girl with an ice cream.

_____ you can see the sea – and a boat. _____ there's a little

brown dog. _____ of the picture there are two children with a ball.

_____ of the postcard it says '*… to sunny Cornwall!*'

3 LISTENING The Muddles ▸ *pp. 10–11* 🎧2

a) *The Muddles have got six children:* **Max**, **Micky**, **Molly**, **Millie**, **Minnie** *and* **Maggie**. *But who's who? Listen and write the names in the boxes.*

b) *Now describe the photo. Use:* **between**, **in front of**,…

Max is _____

_____

_____

_____

_____

Now you

*Where are these things in your room: window, bed, wardrobe, desk/table, chair, clock, lamp? Use **behind**, **between**,*
*in front of, **near**, **next to** and **under**. Write at least five sentences.*

The window is between my bed and my desk.

_____

_____

_____

_____

_____

4 PRONUNCIATION   Vowel sounds   ▶ *p. 12* 🎧 3

*Listen and say the words. Colour the CDs with the same sound **red** [ɜ:], **green** [ɪə] or **blue** [eə].*

girl [ɜ:]   stairs   year   work   their   dear
ear [ɪə]   learn   here   wear   were   near
share [eə]   first   early   clear   where   turn

5 REVISION   How were your holidays? (Simple past: be)   ▶ *p. 12* • *GF 1a (p. 127)*

*Complete the dialogue with **was**, **were**, **wasn't** or **weren't**.*

How were your
holidays, Sophie?

Prunella   Where _____ you all?

Sophie   We _____ on the island
of Majorca.

Prunella   _____ it boring without me?

Sophie   No, it _____ , Prunella.
We _____ in a villa with our
own pool.

Prunella   _____ your room nice, like our room at home?

Sophie   Yes, the rooms _____ big, but my room
_____ very nice.

Prunella   And _____ there any very nice poltergeists in it, like me?

Sophie   No, there _____ , Prunella. No poltergeists.

Prunella   Oh, so your holidays _____ very good…

0605

6 WORDS   Find the new word   ▶ *p. 12*

First write the missing word, then write the letter. The letters give you the answer to the question.

1 It was Ananda's first time on a …   *plane* _____ (4)   *N*

2 American English for 'lift':   _____ (3) _____

3 Ananda and Dilip … there together.   _____ (4) _____

4 American English for 'underground':   _____ (6) _____

5 The subway is fast, but not …   _____ (7) _____

6 The … was great – sun all the time.   _____ (7) _____

7 They … the lift to the top of the Empire State Building.   _____ (4) _____

Question: Where did they go? – To _____ .

7 PRONUNCIATION   Which letters can't your hear?   ▶ *p. 12* 🎧 4

Listen and say the words. Which letters can't you hear? Cross them out (✗).

b X i l d i n g	c u p b o a r d	c l o t h e s
i s l a n d	k n e e	t a l k
h o u r	w h o	w h a t
w a l k	c l i m b	w r o n g
k n o w	S c i e n c e	w r i t e

8 REVISION   A verb snake (Simple past: regular forms)   ▸ p. 12 • GF 1a (p. 127)

Find the regular verbs and write them in the simple past form.

stayed, _____

0808 _____

9 WRITING   Boring! (Linking words and phrases)   ▸ p. 12 • SF (p. 123)

Tim's homework was: 'Write a story about a boring Saturday afternoon'. Can you write Tim's story?
Use simple past forms from exercise 8. You can change the order. Use time phrases too: First, then, after that, an
hour later, … Ideas: football, watch kids, weather, rainy, help mum, clean bike, tidy room, wash car, …

It was a boring Saturday afternoon, so I walked to the park with a

friend. First we played _____

_____

_____

_____

_____

_____

_____

10 Find the verbs (Simple past: irregular forms)   ▶ p. 13 • GF 1b (p. 127)

a) *Find the infinitive and the simple past form. Write two lists.*

k	m	l	p	s	a	p	r	u	n
s	e	e	g	r	h	m	o	n	i
t	e	d	c	o	m	e	f	n	h
o	t	s	k	d	b	t	a	k	e
o	r	i	d	e	m	y	s	w	a
k	a	w	g	v	h	h	a	k	r
c	n	m	o	f	l	e	w	m	d
a	p	g	d	l	k	a	t	e	g
m	l	e	f	y	t	r	g	n	o
e	a	t	g	s	p	w	e	n	t

0910

Infinitive	Simple past
see	saw
_____	_____
_____	_____
_____	_____
_____	_____
_____	_____
_____	_____
_____	_____
_____	_____
_____	_____

b) *Now read what Florian says about a day in the holidays. Complete with simple past forms from a).*

One day in the holidays I _____ to a lake with my dad. We _____ our bikes and _____ some cheese sandwiches for lunch. We _____ a nice place for a picnic, so we _____ our sandwiches under a tree. In the afternoon we _____ two boys with a dog and a kite. The dog wanted to get[1] the kite, but it was windy, so the kite _____ in the sky for at least ten minutes. Then suddenly it _____ down – right on Dad's head.

[1]get [get] *kriegen*

11 WORDS Find the words ▶ p. 13

Find seven words and use them in the sentences.

ness	ing	de	ther	cafe	be	ru	ei
fore	idays	am	busi	Build	azing	hol	teria

1 In the break the students met in the *cafeteria*_____ .

2 They talked about the _____ .

3 Ananda said New York was _____ .

4 She liked the Empire State _____ a lot.

5 Dilip flew back a week _____ Ananda.

6 Lesley, the new girl, was _____ .

7 She said to Sophie, 'Mind your own _____ .'

8 Sophie answered, 'I didn't want to come to Bristol _____ .'

12 REVISION What don't they do? (Simple present: negative statements) ▶ p. 13

*The Muddles children don't always do what their parents say. Write sentences with **doesn't/don't**.*

clean her teeth · eat their breakfast · shout · *have a shower* · wash her face · make their beds

Max:  Max doesn't always have a shower._____

Millie:  _____

Maggie and Minnie:  _____

Millie:  _____

Molly and Micky:  _____

Mr and Mrs Muddles: _____

at their children – but today ...!

13 REVISION Poor Barnabas (Simple past: negative statements) ▸ p. 13 • GF 2 (p. 128)

Barnabas didn't have good holidays. Read why. Write the verbs in the simple past.

I *didn't go* _____ (not go) to Italy with Tim and the Baxters. Tim _____ (not take) me.

But I _____ (not stay) at home with the neighbours. I stayed with Aunt Mildred.

She has got a big, old house – and a big, scary dog. The dog _____ (not play) with me and he

_____ (not give) me his food. I was a good pet, but Aunt Mildred _____ (not talk)

to me much. I _____ (not sit) on her sofa and I was so nice to her.

On the first day I took a nice dead mouse into the house for her. I put it on the kitchen table,

but she _____ (not like) it. I don't know why, because it was a very big, dead mouse ...

1113

14 PRONUNCIATION Sounds ▸ p. 14 🎧5

Listen to the words and match them to the correct sounds.

amazing	[dɪˈskrɪpʃn]	nothing	[əˈbrɔːd]
description	[əˈmeɪzɪŋ]	subway	[mɪˈsteɪk]
remember	[ˈɪtəli]	person	[dɪˈgriː]
caravan	[ˈdeɪndʒərəs]	abroad	[ˈnʌθɪŋ]
dangerous	[rɪˈmembə]	degree	[ˈpɜːsn]
Italy	[ˈkærəvæn]	mistake	[ˈsʌbweɪ]

15 REVISION   Do you like parties? (Simple present: yes/no questions) ▶ p. 14

There's an American boy in your Art Club. Ask questions about him and his sister.

1 like parties? <u>*Do you like parties? Does your sister like parties too?*</u>

2 do sport? _____

3 make models? _____

4 read comics? _____

16 The first day (Simple past: yes/no questions and short answers) ▶ p. 14 • GF 3 (p. 128)

Read A2 and A4 (pp. 13–14) in your student's book again. Then match.

1 Did Ananda and Sophie talk to Lesley?   No, they didn't.

2 Did Lesley talk to the girls?   No, he didn't.

3 Did Jack eat a chicken burger?   No, she didn't.

4 Did Dan get angry?   Yes, they did.

5 Did the girls go outside?   Yes, he did.

1216 *6* Did Lesley say 'Mind your own business'?   Yes, she did.

Rhyme time

A new school year
and lots to do,
New students, books,
new timetable too.
It's fun to laugh and
make new friends,
But I'm always happy
when the school day
ends...

17 Questions for Ananda (Simple past: yes/no questions) ▶ p. 14 • GF 3 (p. 128)

Ananda's mum asked Ananda lots of questions about the first day of school. What did she ask?

1 you – see your friends? <u>*Did you see your friends?*</u>

2 they – talk about their holidays? _____

3 they – ask you about New York? _____

4 Mr Kingsley – give you the new timetable? _____

5 you – use new books? _____

1217 *6* the teachers – give you homework? _____

Just for fun

I took my dog to see the new *Harry Potter* film.

Really? That's amazing! Did he like it?

Yes, he did. And it's amazing, because he didn't like the book.

CINEMAX

Harry Potter

18 **More questions** (Simple past: questions) ▶ p. 14 • GF 3 (p. 128)

*Emily's cousin asked her lots of questions about the holidays. Look at Emily's answers. Write her cousin's questions with **Where**, **What**, **Who**, **How**, **How long**.*

Questions:

Emily's answers:

1 *Where did you go?* _____

We went to Majorca.

2 _____

We went there by plane, of course.

3 _____

We stayed for two weeks.

4 _____

We stayed in a villa near the sea.

5 _____

We went swimming, we played volleyball on the
beach, we went shopping…

1318

6 _____

I met a very nice French boy.

19 **Who called who after school?** (Subject/Object questions) ▶ p. 15 • GF 4 (p. 129)

a) *Write two questions each with **Who**… Then write the answers (names only). You need the numbers for b).*

Becky | Marie | Lucy | Tim | Florian | Jeff

Ask about…

Tim: *Who called Tim?* _____ *Jeff* ____ *5* ____

Who did Tim call? _____ *Florian* ____ *7* ____

Becky: _____ _____ ____

_____ _____ ____

Florian: _____ _____ ____

_____ _____ ____

Lucy: _____ _____ ____

_____ _____ ____

b) *Now write the numbers on the photos next to your answers. It's Tim's telephone number. Is it A, B, C or D?*

A 57382053   B 57323058   C 57308523   D 57308532

20 WORKING WITH THE TEXT   Saved!   ▶ pp. 22–23

a) *Read the story on pp. 22–23 of your student's book again. Write the missing words.*
The letters in the boxes give you a place name from the story. ▶ *What is it?*

1 Dan looked out to [s] ___ ___ .

2 Jody didn't know about the [ ] ___ d ___ ___ ___ .

3 Jody was a good ___ ___ [ ] ___ ___ ___ ___ ___ .

4 Dan saw Jody ___ ___ [ ] .

5 A ___ ___ f [ ] ___ ___ ___ came
to pull Jody out of the sea.

6 The lifeboatmen – and the twins –
[ ] ___ ___ ___ ___ Jody's life.

▶ The place name is ___ ___ ___ ___ ___ ___ .

b) *Put the pictures in the right order. Write 1–6 in the boxes.*

c) *Now you are Dan. Write a letter to Grandma Shaw about Jody. Use the simple past and write in your exercise book.*

first – have breakfast – caravan • after breakfast – go swimming • then – see – Jody – beach •
we – play – football – other people, but – be worried because Jody – be – so far away • she – not know –
tides • man with binoculars – see that Jody – be in trouble • Dad – call – lifeboat – mobile •
a few minutes later – lifeboat – come – St Ives • men – pull – Jody – out of – sea • she – be – OK •
we – go – St Ives – dad – see her

Dear Grandma

I must tell you what happened yesterday. Well, first we had breakfast in the caravan…

What can you do now?

1 What's the weather like?

1 It's _____.

2 _____

3 _____

4 _____

1501

2 That's wrong!

*These sentences are wrong. Write them with **didn't**.*

1 Lesley tried to be nice. _____

2 She wanted to come to Bristol. _____

3 Jack flew to New York. _____

1502 4 Jo ran to get help for Jody. _____

3 Ask Ananda questions.

Read Ananda's answers, then write your questions.

1 _____ – We went to New York.

2 _____ – We stayed for two weeks.

3 _____ – It was really hot on most days.

1503 4 _____ – Lots of things. We went up the Empire State Building, we went shopping, we went on a boat trip.

4 Describe the picture.

Where are they? Use: **between, behind, on the right, on the left**

1 Ali is _____.

2 Sue is _____.

3 Pat is _____.

1504 4 Ed is _____.

16 points

● Now you

1505
1506

In your exercise book, write at least four sentences about the first day of school after the holidays. What did you do? What didn't you do? Ideas: **get a new timetable, see your old friends, do a lot of work, talk about the holidays, get lots of homework**

Unit 2 What money can buy

1 STUDY SKILLS   Learning words – Step 2   ▶ pp. 26–27 • SF (p. 115)

a) First, find four group words from the box and write them at the top of the lists. Then write the other words in the correct groups.

> months • July • knee • skirt • clothes • cloudy • shirt • shoulder • weather • countries • Scotland • leg • body • March • New Zealand • stormy • trousers • sunny • England • toes • foggy • May • blouse • December • Germany

1 months	2	3	4	5
July				

1601

b) Now find group words for these things.

1 | collecting things | reading | playing the guitar | making models | _____
2 | pencil case | ruler | felt tip | rubber | _____
3 | food | guests | invitations | presents | _____

2 LISTENING   Becky's friends   ▶ pp. 26–27 🎧 6

Becky is talking about her four best friends. Look, listen and tick (✓) the correct four boxes.

3 WORDS   Our favourite clothes   ▶ pp. 26–27

a) *What are Tim and Becky wearing today? Write the clothes words.*

cap

1703

b) *Now write about what they are wearing. Use colour words and long, short, a pair of …*

Tim is wearing a blue cap, a red

4 WORDS   make **or** do?   ▶ p. 28

a) *Match.*

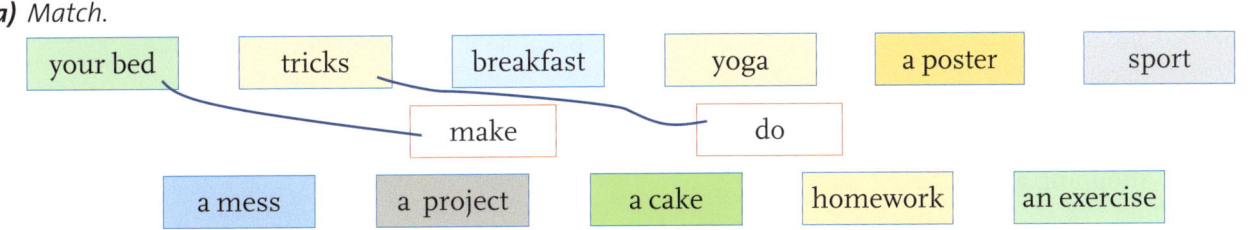

| your bed | tricks | breakfast | yoga | a poster | sport |

make   do

| a mess | a project | a cake | homework | an exercise |

b) *Now fill in the right forms.*

doing • do (2x) • made • make • makes • making

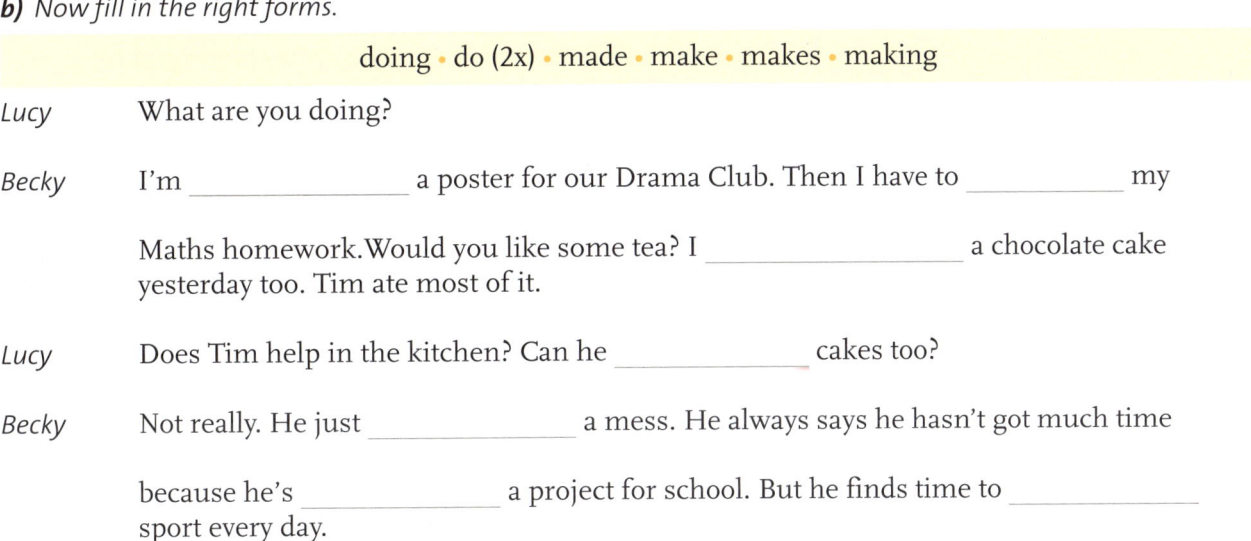

Lucy   What are you doing?

Becky   I'm _____ a poster for our Drama Club. Then I have to _____ my

Maths homework. Would you like some tea? I _____ a chocolate cake
yesterday too. Tim ate most of it.

Lucy   Does Tim help in the kitchen? Can he _____ cakes too?

Becky   Not really. He just _____ a mess. He always says he hasn't got much time

because he's _____ a project for school. But he finds time to _____
sport every day.

1704

5 It isn't mine (Possessive pronouns) ▶ *p. 28* • *GF 5 (p. 130)*

Tim wants to go to the park with Florian, but it's cold and windy.
Use mine, yours, his, hers, ours, theirs, yours.

Mrs Baxter Tim, it's windy. Take your cap. Here it is.

Tim   But Mum, that isn't (my cap) _____mine_____ .

     Florian, is it (your cap) _____?

Florian No, it isn't. (My cap) _____ is blue.

Tim   Oh, so it isn't (our cap) _____ . Then whose is it?

Florian Well, Nick has got a cap like that. Maybe it's (his cap) _____.

Tim   Becky has got a red cap too. Maybe it's (her cap) _____. And the neighbours'

     twins have got red caps. Maybe it's one of (their caps) _____.

Florian Try it on, Tim. Does it fit? Hey! It looks great! Now it's (your cap) _____!

Tim   The wind! Oh, no! Where's the cap now?

1805 Florian Look! It's up there, in that big tree! So now it's nobody's cap …

6 REVISION What did you do? (Simple past) ▶ *p. 28* • *GF 1–3 (pp. 127–128)*

Fill in the correct form of the simple past.

Sophie When we were on holiday, I _____went_____ (go) swimming every day.

Prunella Where _____did you go_____ (you/go) swimming? In the sea?

Sophie No, we _____ (not go) in the sea because it was often very windy. We _____
     (like) our pool in the garden.

Prunella And what _____ (Emily/do) all day? (she/go) _____
     shopping a lot?

     What _____ (she/buy)? Lots of presents for her friends?

Sophie Well, _____ (she/not buy) presents. Just clothes, I think.
     Tops, a pair of jeans, a blouse, some trousers, a skirt, some make-up …

Prunella Oh! Really! But you _____ (buy) presents for your friends, Sophie.

1806 And _____ (you/buy) a present for me?

Just for fun

A: What are you doing?
B: I'm eating these chips.
A: But those chips were mine.
B: Yes, right. They were yours.

Now you

What did you do in the holidays? Where did you go? Did you go shopping? What did you buy?
Write at least three sentences in your exercise book.

7 REVISION   We need some milk (some and any)   ▶ *p. 29*

What do Dan and Jo need to make these things? Write sentences with some *or* any.

1 tea:

They need some tea and some milk. They don't need any _____

2 fish and chips:

_____

3 fruit salad:

_____

4 cheese sandwiches:

_____

8 Does anybody know …? (some and any compounds)   ▶ *p. 29* • *GF 6 (p. 130)*

Complete with: something – anything, somebody – anybody, somewhere – anywhere

Tim   Does _____ know where my French book is?

Becky   Sorry, I don't know _____ about your things.

Tim   Well, _____ must know what happened to it.

        I can't find it _____ .

Becky   Maybe it's under your bed – or in your wardrobe?

Tim   Ha, ha! You're mad.

Becky   Well, it must be _____ . Ask Mum. Or maybe one of your friends knows

        _____ about it.

Tim   My friends haven't got it. Who wants two French books? One is enough!
        Now, where's my sandwich box for school? (Opens the fridge door.) Oh, no! Mum put my
        French book in the fridge with my sandwiches.
        Mum! It says 'French verbs' not 'French cheese'!

9 PRONUNCIATION   Sounds at the end of words (Consonants)   ▸ p. 29 🎧 7

Listen and write. Which sound do you hear at the end of the word?

[b] or [p]?

job [dʒɒ __b__]   club [klʌ ___]   stop [stɒ ___]

drop [drɒ ___]   Rob [rɒ ___]   cap [kæ ___]

[g] or [k] ?

bag [bæ __g__]   back [bæ ___]   leg [le ___]

fog [fɒ ___]   look [lʊ ___]   big [bɪ ___]

[d] or [t]?

card [kɑ: __d__]   looked [lʊk ___]   told [təʊl ___]

dropped [drɒp ___]   heard [hɜ: ___]   helped [help ___]

2009

'b' like Barnabas?

or 'p' like Polly?'

10 How much ...? (much/many – more – most)   ▸ p. 29

a) *Complete with **much** or **many**.*

Florian   I don't get _____ __much__ _____ pocket money, but I don't buy _____ __many__ _____ things.

Tim   I don't need _____ money because Mum buys my clothes and

stuff for school. I don't buy _____ comics now because my cousin gives me his. I buy chocolate, but

not _____ .

Florian   Well, I don't buy _____ sweets, but I buy lots of ice cream in summer – and that's expensive.

Rhyme time

Fun with my pet,
A day with friends,
I'm always sad
When a good time ends.
I don't need much money,
Because, you see,
The things I like
Are always free.

b) [Extra] *Now make comparisons with **more** and **the most**.*

I buy a sports magazine every week, a comic and a computer magazine. I usually save two pounds of my pocket money.

I buy a car magazine, a football magazine, a comic and a music magazine every week. I don't save much, maybe a pound.

I buy a computer magazine and a pop magazine. I save three pounds every week.

Florian   Lucy   Tim

Lucy *doesn't buy many magazines*. Florian _____

than Lucy, but Tim _____ .

2010
2011   Florian _____ *saves* _____ than Tim, but Lucy _____ .

11 PRONUNCIATION   Stress (Betonung) ▶ *p. 29* 🎧 8

Is the stress in the same place in German and in English? Listen to the words and write Y (= Yes) or N (= No).

1	hamster	–	Hamster	_Y_		
2	information	–	Information	_N_		
3	jacket	–	Jackett	_____		
4	project	–	Projekt	_____		
5	picnic	–	Picknick	_____		
6	pullover	–	Pullover	_____		

7	music	–	Musik	_____
8	judo	–	Judo	_____
9	moment	–	Moment	_____
10	problem	–	Problem	_____
11	photo	–	Foto	_____
12	person	–	Person	_____

12 Who's going to do what? (going to-future) ▶ *p. 30* • *GF 7 (p. 131)*

Read the speech bubbles and write what they are going to do this evening.
*Use **going to** and **call**, **buy**, **play**, **wash**.*

1   I think Maggie is going to _____ .

2   _____

3   _____

4   _____

13 Compare (Comparison of adjectives) ▶ *p. 31* • *GF 8a/c (pp. 132–133)*

Write sentences with ... than ...

1    English, Maths (easy):

Maths is easier than English. / English is easier than Maths.

2    a fish, a hamster (nice):

_____

3    tennis, table tennis (good):

_____

4    a cat, a mouse (big):

_____

2213

5   spy stories, detective stories (scary):

_____

14 WORDS   Pairs ▶ *p. 32*

Which of Prunella's plates go together? Match, colour and write pairs.

start – finish _____

_____

_____

15 READING Dogs ▶ *p. 32*

a) *Read about the four dogs* Sam*,* James*,* Boss *and* Pluto*. Who's who? Write their names under the pictures.*

Wuff!
Wuff! Wuff!

_____   _____   _____   _____

Sam is the smallest dog, but he has got the longest hair and the longest ears. He's a sweet dog.
Boss is louder than all the other dogs. He makes lots of noise all the time – in the park,
in the garden, in the house. The neighbours aren't very happy. James has got the biggest head
and very short legs. He isn't as pretty as the others and he isn't as fast, but he's a very nice dog
because he never makes problems. Pluto is the fastest of all the dogs. He has got the longest body
and the longest legs. He can run for miles in the park – like the wind. One dog has got a long body
with short hair and short legs. He looks really funny, almost like a sausage.

2315

b) *Whose dogs are they? Match the dogs to the kids.*

Ali:

My dog is the fastest.
His name is _____ .

Sue:

My dog is the smallest.
His name is _____ .

Nick:

My dog is the loudest.
His name is _____ .

Ed:

My dog is the slowest – and
he isn't the prettiest, but for me he's the greatest.
His name is _____ .

And who's
the cleverest cat you
know?

Now you

Which dog do you like? Why?
How is he different from the others?
Write at least two sentences in your exercise book.

16 WRITING   Millie, Minnie and Molly (Comparison of adjectives)   ▶ *p. 32 • GF 8a/c (pp. 132–133)*

Compare Millie, Minnie and Molly Muddles.
Write five sentences or more.
Use: young, old, big, small, long, short, dark, funny

Ideas: Who is younger/bigger than the others?
Who is the oldest? Who has got the longest hair,
the darkest hair? Who is the funniest?

Millie, 4   Minnie, 2   Molly, 6

Millie is older than Minnie, but she's younger than Molly. Molly is the oldest and Minnie

2416

17 Which is the most exciting? (Comparison of adjectives)   ▶ *p. 32 • GF 8a–c (pp. 132–133)*

What do you think? Write sentences.

1 exciting: A    B    C

I think B is the most exciting.

2 dangerous: A    B    C

3 expensive: A    B    C

4 interesting: A    B    C

2417

18 WORDS You can see films here ▶ p. 32

Complete the puzzle. ▶ *What's the word in the green boxes?*

1 You can see films here.

2 Not 'expensive' but …

3 Another word for 'terrible' is …

4 The … in this café is very slow.

5 Jack needs a new … of trainers.

6 Ananda is writing a … to her grandma.

7 When you can use paper again, it's …

You can buy cheap things here: ▶ _____ shop.

19 MEDIATION Shopping for trainers ▶ p. 32 • SF (p. 125)

Florian is in a shoe shop in Bristol with his German cousin Heike.

Heike	Sag der Verkäuferin, ich brauche ein Paar neue Turnschuhe. Sie können billig sein.
Florian	*Excuse me, she needs a new pair* _____
Shop assistant	Ask her what size and what colour she would like. We have got a lot of new models.
Florian	_____
Heike	Ich bin nicht sicher. Sag ihr, ich möchte einige anprobieren. Sie haben schöne Schuhe.
Florian	_____
Shop assistant	What about blue? We have got some nice new models in pink too. But they're expensive. Maybe she doesn't want to spend so much money.
Florian	_____
Shop assistant	She can try on these. They're really nice. It's the last pair in this colour.
Florian	_____
Heike	Sie passen nicht. Sie sind viel zu eng. Und sie sind ein bisschen zu teuer. Hat sie andere?
Florian	_____

(Twenty minutes later.)

Florian	Heike, komm jetzt. Du hast schon vierzehn Paar Turnschuhe anprobiert.
Heike	Klar. Gehen wir. Ich habe sowieso nicht genug Geld.

20 WORKING WITH THE TEXT   The Clothes Project   ▸ *pp. 40–41*

a) Read pp. 40–41 of your student's book again. What's right? Tick (✔) A, B or C.

1 Sophie and Jack are working on the project at   A   school.   B   Jack's house.   C   Sophie's house.

2 When they talk about the project, Jack has   A   lots of ideas.   B   no ideas.   C   only one good idea.

3 Who had the idea for a fashion show?   A   Jack and Sophie.   B   Lesley and Ananda.

   C   Rachel and Tom.

4 Who went upstairs and into the attic first?   A   Prunella.   B   Jack.   C   Sophie.

5 What did Prunella drop?   A   A plate and a hat.   B   A plate, a hat and a pair of shoes.

   C   A plate, a hat and three pairs of shoes.

6 The dress from the wardrobe is   A   long and white.   B   short and blue.   C   long and blue.

b) What goes together? Match and write under the correct pictures.

> Something scary • Tea first • Poor Grandma's plates • Up to the attic •
> What about a fashion show? • In Grandma's wardrobe

What?!
Me in a fashion show? No way!

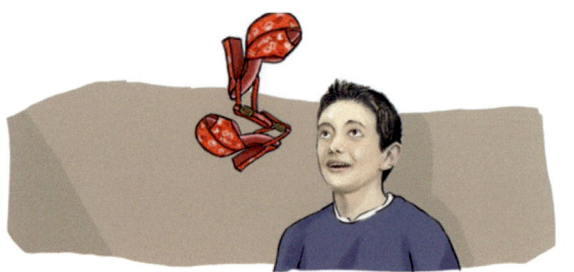

c) Now retell the story in about eight sentences. Use the simple past and write in your exercise book.

1 Clothes: write the names.

What can you do now?

1 _____

2 _____

3 _____

4 _____

5 _____

6 _____

2701

2 Find group words for these things.

1 trainers • shorts • sports bag • T-shirt _____

2 cinema • shopping • computer games _____

3 hair • nose • eyes • ears _____

2702 4 dress • shorts • trousers • pullover _____

3 Whose is it? Complete with _mine_, _yours_,...

Tim   Is this old jacket _____ , Becky?

Becky   No, it isn't _____ . Ask Mum. Maybe it's _____ . Or ask Dad.

2703 Tim   Ask Dad? It isn't _____ . It's pink with little white rabbits!

4 Compare with _than_.

1 Art – Music: easy

_____

2 detective stories – animal stories: exciting

_____

3 Sophie – Emily: nice

2704 _____

4 the Simpsons – Mr Bean: funny

_____

5 a summer holiday – a holiday in the snow: good

_____

6 a boring Sunday – a long school day: bad

_____

20 points

● **Now you**

2705
2706 *Write about shopping. What do you buy with your pocket money? Do you spend much money on sweets, drinks, magazines? What do you spend most money on? Do you save much? Write at least five sentences in your exercise book.*

Jetzt kann ich ...   Sehr gut!   OK   Verbessern!

HÖREN: Ich kann ...

... die Arbeitsanweisungen, Fragen und Erklärungen meiner Lehrerin/ meines Lehrers verstehen.   ☐ ☐ ☐

... verstehen, was im Unterricht von meinen Mitschülern/-innen gesagt, gefragt und gespielt wird.   ☐ ☐ ☐

... das Wichtigste aus Hörtexten der Units Welcome back, 1 und 2 meines Buchs sowie die Listening-Aufgaben meines Workbooks verstehen.   ☐ ☐ ☐

... die Vokabeln der Units Welcome back, 1 und 2 verstehen.   ☐ ☐ ☐

SPRECHEN: Ich kann ...

... im Unterricht frei erzählen und fragen, auch wenn ich kleine Fehler mache.   ☐ ☐ ☐

... korrekt und flüssig die Wörter der Units Welcome back, 1 und 2 aussprechen und anwenden.   ☐ ☐ ☐

... mich an Rollenspielen und an gespielten Szenen aus meinem Buch beteiligen.   ☐ ☐ ☐

... über das Wetter sprechen.   ☐ ☐ ☐

... mit dem *simple past* sagen, was ich gestern/letzte Woche/in den Ferien getan habe und wo ich gewesen bin.   ☐ ☐ ☐

... über Geld, Taschengeld, Einkäufe, das Ausgeben und Sparen von Geld sprechen.   ☐ ☐ ☐

... die Vokallaute [ɜː], [ɪə] und [eə] voneinander unterscheiden und richtig aussprechen.   ☐ ☐ ☐

LESEN: Ich kann ...

... eine Postkarte oder einen kurzen Brief auf Englisch lesen und verstehen.   ☐ ☐ ☐

... eine Karte von Europa verstehen.   ☐ ☐ ☐

... die längeren Erzähltexte und Dialoge der Units Welcome back, 1 und 2 lesen und verstehen.   ☐ ☐ ☐

... die längeren Erzähltexte und Dialoge der Units Welcome back, 1 und 2 ohne Probleme laut vorlesen.   ☐ ☐ ☐

... kurze Sachtexte verstehen.   ☐ ☐ ☐

SCHREIBEN: Ich kann ...

... eine Postkarte oder einen kurzen Brief an Freunde oder Verwandte schreiben.   ☐ ☐ ☐

... Tagebucheinträge schreiben.   ☐ ☐ ☐

... darüber schreiben, was ich in den Sommerferien gemacht habe.   ☐ ☐ ☐

... die Wörter der Units Welcome back, 1 und 2 richtig schreiben.   ☐ ☐ ☐

LAND UND LEUTE: Ich ...

... habe etwas über Cornwall und New York gelernt.   ☐ ☐ ☐

... weiß, wie britische Schüler ihre Freizeit verbringen.   ☐ ☐ ☐

Jetzt kann ich ...

	Sehr gut!	OK	Verbessern!

GRAMMATIKVERSTÄNDNIS: Ich kann ...

... die Verbformen des *simple present* (z.B. *play*, *make*) und des *simple past* (z.B. *played*, *made*) erkennen und voneinander unterscheiden. ☐ ☐ ☐

... mit dem *simple past* ausdrücken, was ich oder andere zu einem gewissen Zeitpunkt in der Vergangenheit gemacht haben (z.B. *Yesterday I worked/ saw/bought ...*). ☐ ☐ ☐

... mit *mine, yours, his* usw. ausdrücken, was jemandem gehört. ☐ ☐ ☐

... Dinge und Personen vergleichen. Dazu steigere ich Adjektive mit *-er/-est* oder mit *more/most* (z.B. *big, bigger, biggest, expensive, more expensive, most expensive*). ☐ ☐ ☐

VOKABELVERSTÄNDNIS: Ich kann ...

... Wörter, die das Wetter beschreiben (z.B. *sunny, rainy, cloudy*), richtig verwenden. ☐ ☐ ☐

... viele Ländernamen (z.B. *Italy, Scotland, Wales*) richtig verwenden. ☐ ☐ ☐

... 'Ferien'-Wörter (z.B. *plane, fly, beach, sea, mountains, lake*) richtig verwenden. ☐ ☐ ☐

... Wörter für Kleidungstücke und Schuhe (z.B. *trousers, skirt, trainers*) richtig verwenden. ☐ ☐ ☐

... mehrere Präpositonen des Ortes (z.B. *behind, next to*) richtig verwenden. ☐ ☐ ☐

SKILLS – LERNEN UND ARBEITEN: Ich ...

... kann Bilder beschreiben, indem ich sage, wo sich etwas genau befindet. Dazu verwende ich z.B. *in the middle/background/foreground*. ☐ ☐ ☐

... kann Wörter nach einem Oberbegriff in Gruppen sammeln und ordnen. ☐ ☐ ☐

... kann eine Mindmap erstellen, um Ideen zu sammeln und zu ordnen. ☐ ☐ ☐

... kann mit einem Partner oder einer Partnerin und in einer Gruppe arbeiten. ☐ ☐ ☐

... weiß, dass ich bei der Mediation nur das Wesentliche übersetzen und weitergeben muss. ☐ ☐ ☐

WAS ICH FÜR MEIN ENGLISCHLERNEN GETAN HABE: Ich habe ...

	häufig	manchmal	nie
... am Unterrichtsgespräch aktiv teilgenommen.	☐	☐	☐
... ein Vokabelheft oder eine Vokabelkartei geführt.	☐	☐	☐
... mit Mindmaps Ideen gesammelt und geordnet.	☐	☐	☐
... mit dem Grammar File in meinem Buch gearbeitet.	☐	☐	☐
... mit dem Skills File in meinem Buch gearbeitet.	☐	☐	☐

WIE ICH MICH VERBESSERN KÖNNTE: Ich könnte ...

... den Unterrichtsstoff jeden Tag zu Hause kurz wiederholen. ☐

... Texte aus meinem Buch zu Hause laut lesen. ☐

... kurze Hörtexte nachsprechen und auswendig lernen. ☐

... schwierige Wörter häufiger abschreiben. ☐

... mindestens ein Gedicht/einen Reim auswendig lernen. ☐

... das Grammar File und das Skills File mehr nutzen und die vorgeschlagenen Aufgaben bearbeiten. ☐

Unit 3 Animals in the city

1 WORDS Find the animals ► *pp. 44–45*

a) *Write the correct names of the animals.*

f x o	fox	p w e o c o k d r e	_____
r g o f	_____	g h e h d g e o	_____
e r d e	_____	r s u l r e q i	_____

3001
3002

b) *Find the animals. Write sentences with* on the right, on the left, in the middle (of the picture), at the top, at the bottom, in the background,...

1 There's a *frog at the bottom on the left.* _____

2 There's a _____ .

3 _____

4 _____

5 _____

6 _____

c) *Choose your favourite animal in a) and write at least three sentences about it in your exercise book.*
Ideas: My favourite animal is the ... It's big/small/fast/slow/quiet/dangerous/ ... It lives in ... It likes ...

2 What will they need? (will-future) ► p. 46 • GF 9 (p. 134)

Tim and Florian want to go on a bike trip to a lake. The weather will be hot. What do you think they'll need?
Write sentences with: **They'll need** *... or* **They won't need** *...*

1 *They'll need some sandwiches.* _____

2 *They won't need* _____

3 _____

4 _____

5 _____

3102 6 _____

3 When will you be home? (will-future: questions) ► p. 46 • GF 9 (p. 134)

Emily wants to go to a party. Her mum asks her some questions. Write the questions with a question word
(**when/how/who**) + **will**. *Choose the correct verb:* **be, finish, get, call, start, take**

1 *When will the party start?* _____ — At about seven o'clock, I think.

2 *How many kids* _____ — About fifteen kids will be there.

3 _____ — Not later than ten or ten-thirty.

4 _____ home? — By train, with three of the other girls.

5 _____ — Gemma's dad will take us to the station.

3103
3104 6 _____ — I'll call when we get on the train.

● Now you

How old will you be on your next birthday? Do you think you'll have a party? How many friends will you invite?
What will you have to eat? Will you play games? Write at least five sentences in your exercise book.
Start with: **I think I'll** *...,* **I/We probably won't** *...*

4 Baby hedgehogs ... (Conditional sentences 1)   ▶ *p. 47* • *GF 10 (p. 135)*

*If you find a baby hedgehog, what will you do? What won't you do? Write sentences with **I'll (I will)** and **I won't**.*

① give   ② give   ③ keep/warm   ④ give   ⑤ take to

If I find a baby hedgehog, ...

1 *I'll give it water.* _____

2 *I won't* _____

3204 3 _____

4 _____

5 _____

5 Tim's mum always says ... (Conditional sentences 1)   ▶ *p. 47* • *GF 10 (p. 135)*

*Match the sentence parts. Then write sentences with **If ...***

1	eat lots of sweets	be ill
2	talk in class	get bad teeth
3	go to bed late	be tired tomorrow
4	watch scary DVDs	have problems with your teachers
5	eat too many hamburgers	have bad dreams

1 *If you eat lots of sweets, you'll get bad teeth.* _____

2 _____

3 _____

4 _____

5 _____

6 What will you do if ...? (Conditional sentences 1)   ▶ *p. 47* • *GF 10 (p. 135)*

*Complete the sentences with **I'll/we'll** + a verb or with the simple present.*
Use the ideas in brackets ( ) or your own ideas.

1 If the weather is good on Saturday, I _*'ll go to the park. / 'll go to the shops.*_ (park)

2 If my friend comes this afternoon, we _____ . (DVDs)

3 I'll buy a CD next week if _____ . (enough money)

4 I'll go to my friend's party if _____ . (an invitation)

o 7 WORDS   A puzzle   ▶ *p. 47*

Write the answers in the puzzle. ▶ *Then find the new word in the orange boxes.*

1 Foxes and squirrels are … animals.

2 … are really pretty animals.

3 Ananda found two hedgehog …

4 'Take the hedgehogs to an animal clinic as … as you can.'

5 If you give hedgehogs milk, they will get …

6 Keep them warm with a hot-water …

7 Last night the babies … in a warm box.

1	2	3	4	5	6	7
		a				
	r				l	t
d		n				

▶ You can find a lot about animals on the Animal Hotline _____.

8 WORDS   The odd one out   ▶ *p. 47*

Find the odd one out and write it down. Then write the letters.
▶ *Put the letters in the right order and find the word.*

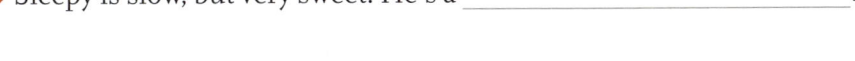

1 mountains   lake   trees   ~~view~~   sea   _____*view*_____   (3)   *e*___

2 shirt   trousers   face   blouse   jacket   _____   (4)   _____

3 fox   deer   squirrel   budgie   mole   _____   (4)   _____

4 car   bike   station   plane   train   _____   (6)   _____

5 church   rubbish   library   museum   school   _____   (7)   _____

6 stormy   foggy   rainy   rudely   cloudy   _____   (3)   _____

7 scary   awful   terrible   amazing   _____   (7)   _____

8 hamster   tortoise   rabbit   guinea pig   hutch   _____   (1)   _____

▶ Sleepy is slow, but very sweet. He's a _____.

Ouch!!!

9 READING   Tim's problem   ▶ *p. 47*

a) Tim is telling Lucy about a problem. Read about the problem.

I've got a friend in the next village. His name is Benny. His birthday is on Thursday and I've got an invitation to go to his party.

I would really like to go because after the party there's a junior disco. But there's a problem. It isn't easy to get to Benny's house. His parents have a nice house with a big garden, but it's at the end of the village. I'll have to go there by bus, because my dad can't take me on that day, and there aren't many buses to the village. I'll have to come home by bus because my dad won't be in Bristol. He'll be in London.

And there's another problem. The last bus from Benny's village goes at 9.30, and the junior disco won't finish before 10 o'clock. If I stay till the end, I won't get the last bus. And I'll have to walk to the bus alone, and it will be dark.

Mum doesn't think that's a good idea. All Benny's friends want to stay till the end of the disco because they don't live far away.

Benny says I can stay the night at his house, but how will I get to school the next morning? I'll have to get up very early. If I don't get the bus, I'll get to school too late for the first lesson. My French teacher will be angry again, and I'll have to do extra homework. Then my friends will go to the cinema without me. I don't know what to do.

b) Right or wrong? Tick (✔) the correct box.

	Right	Wrong
1 Tim has got an invitation to Benny's party.	☐	☐
2 Benny's parents have a nice house with a garden in Bristol.	☐	☐
3 Tim's dad can take him to Benny's house.	☐	☐
4 If Tim stays to the end of the party, he'll get the last bus home.	☐	☐
5 If he doesn't get the last bus, he'll have to stay the night at Benny's house.	☐	☐
6 If he stays at Benny's house, he won't have to get up early.	☐	☐
7 He won't be late for school on the next day.	☐	☐
8 If Tim is late for school, the teacher will give him extra homework.	☐	☐
9 If Tim gets extra homework, he'll have to stay at home in the evening.	☐	☐
10 If he has to stay at home, his friends won't go to the cinema.	☐	☐

*c) What will happen if …? Write five sentences with **If** … about Tim's problem in your exercise book.*

If Tim goes to the party, he'll have to go there by bus.

10 WRITING   Korky (Linking ideas)   ▶ *p. 47*

a) *Your pet dog Korky is ill. Write an e-mail about Korky to a friend.*
Link two sentences with a red or a blue word.

| When After | My dog Korky is eleven years old.
I'm not very happy at the moment.
He must be hungry.
I come home from school.
I took him to the park yesterday.
I feed him.
He's always a happy dog.
We're worried about him. | but
and
because
so | He's my best friend.
Korky is ill.
He doesn't eat his food.
We usually go to the park.
He just sat under a tree and slept.
He usually wants to play with me.
He's very quiet now.
Maybe we'll take him to the animal clinic tomorrow. |

Dear _____

My dog Korky is eleven years old and he's my best friend. _____

I'm not very happy at the moment _____

_____

_____

_____

_____

_____

_____

_____

_____

🖥
3510

b) *Now write at least three more sentences about Korky. Use a red or blue word from a) in each sentence.*

_____

_____

_____

_____

_____

11 At school (Adverbs of manner)　▶ *p. 48 • GF 11a–b, d (p. 136)*

Adjective or adverb? Cross out (✗) the wrong word.

The Bristol kids like school and they're good students too. Sophie usually works (carefully/~~careful~~)
and her work isn't (bad/badly). Ananda learns (quick/quickly) and works (quietly/quiet). Most
of the boys learn (easily/easy) too, but sometimes they are really (horrible/horribly). Mr Kingsley
is always (nicely/nice) to his students, but when they talk (loud/loudly) he's sometimes (angry/angrily).
When he gives the students extra homework, they are suddenly (quiet/quietly) – and not
very (happy/happily).

3611

12 How? (Adverbs of manner)　▶ *p. 48 • GF 11a–b, d (p. 136)*

What are the Muddles' kids doing now, and how? Complete the sentences with adverbs.
Choose from: angrily, dangerously, hungrily, loudly, quickly, terribly

1　Mr Muddles is shouting ___*angrily*___ .

2　Molly is riding her bike _____ .

3　Max is eating _____ .

4　Micky is laughing _____

5　Maggie is dancing _____ .

6　Millie is running _____ .

Now you

How do you do these things? Write sentences with an adverb.
1 eat your breakfast　2 ride your bike　3 dance　4 talk　5 sing　6 paint

_____

_____

_____

_____

_____

_____

13 PRONUNCIATION [f] – [v] – [w] ▶ p. 48 🎧 9

a) *Listen and say the words. Do you hear [f], [v] or [w]? Tick (✔) the right box. Then write the word.*

	1 [f]	2 [v]	3 [w]			1 [f]	2 [v]	3 [w]	
1	☐	☐	✔	water	5	☐	☐	☐	
2	☐	☐	☐		6	☐	☐	☐	
3	☐	☐	☐		7	☐	☐	☐	
4	☐	☐	☐		8	☐	☐	☐	

3713

Count your points: [f] = 1, [v] = 2, [w] = 3. If your answers are correct, you will have 16 points!

b) *Now say these sentences as quickly as you can.*

1 On a foggy Friday in November Fred found fifty-five frogs in the fridge.
2 Last week we visited a family in a very funny village in Wales.
3 When Will visited Vicky and Val the weather was very windy.

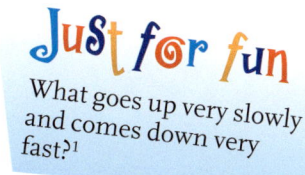

Just for fun
What goes up very slowly and comes down very fast?[1]

14 Jo can run very … (Adverbs of manner) ▶ p. 49 • GF 11 (p. 136)

Write the adverbs in the puzzle and find the new word in the green boxes.

badly	easily	fast	hard	slowly	well

1 Jo loves football. He can run very …

2 Sophie is in the Dance Club. She dances very …

3 Ananda is good at school. She works very …

4 Jack writes stories. He can write them …

5 But Jack hates sports. He plays football …

6 Jo doesn't like Maths. He works too …

▶ And Polly? She sings _____ .

(Puzzle grid with letters **r** and **y** in green boxes)

● Now you

What do you usually do well? What do you often do fast? What do you always do carefully?
What do you sometimes do badly? Write four sentences.

_____

_____

_____

_____

15 LISTENING A walk in the woods   ▶ *p. 49* 🎧 10

a) *Mr Baxter is walking in the woods with Tim and Becky. Listen carefully.*

b) *Now tick (✔) the correct answer, A, B or C. Sometimes more than one answer is correct.*

		A		B		C	
1	Tim is talking …	A	quietly.	B	loudly.	C	quickly.
2	There's a programme on TV tonight about …	A	moles.	B	deer.	C	squirrels.
3	What did Becky see in the woods last year?	A	A fox.	B	A deer.	C	Two deer.
4	Why does a woodpecker make a hole in a tree?	A	To sleep in.	B	To put food in.		
		C	To lay¹ eggs in.				
5	A fast red fox can run … miles an hour.	A	13	B	30	C	33
6	What do foxes eat?	A	Mice.	B	Cats.	C	Fruit.
7	What does Becky see in a tree?	A	A red squirrel.	B	A mole.		
		C	A woodpecker.				
8	Tim says, ' … are cool.'	A	Frogs	B	Hedgehogs		
		C	Moles				
9	Becky likes …	A	deer.	B	frogs.	C	hedgehogs.
10	Tim wants to take frogs home and put them …	A	in the garden.	B	in a fish bowl.		
		C	in a cage.				

¹ lay [leɪ] *legen*

3815

16 STUDY SKILLS Scanning ▶ p. 49 • SF (p. 120)

What do you know about red deer? Read the questions below, then scan the text to find the answers as quickly as you can. Write down your answers.

Description
The red deer is the biggest wild animal in the UK.
In summer they are dark red or brown. In winter
they are dark brown or grey. They can swim well.

How long do they live?
Deer usually live as long as 10 or 15 years.
Deer in parks can live for 20 years.

Their enemies
Many young deer survive only for a few weeks
because the weather is too cold for them.
Sometimes foxes and wild cats kill deer babies for
food. But life is dangerous for older animals too.
Every year cars kill about 40,000 deer on the
roads.

Where do they live?
About 350,000 red deer live wild in Scotland.
They live on the islands near Scotland too. You
can see them in many places, in parks and even
in the mountains. They like to live near lots of
trees, because they can find more food there.
They usually live in groups of 10 to[1] 40 animals,
but sometimes there are more than a hundred
deer in one group.

Baby deer
A deer mother usually has one baby every year, in
May or June. A baby deer is brown and white. It
can stand after only a few minutes and can run
after a few hours. A young deer stays with its
mother till she has another baby.

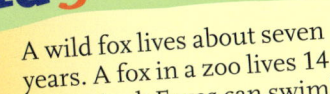
Did you know?
A wild fox lives about seven
years. A fox in a zoo lives 14
years. And: Foxes can swim!

1 What colour are deer in summer?

2 Can deer swim?

3 How long do deer usually live?

4 Deer have enemies. What or who are they?

5 How many deer live in Scotland?

6 How many babies does a mother
have every year?

7 How soon can a baby deer run?

[1] to [tə] hier: *bis*

17 REVISION   Which animal is bigger? (Comparison of adjectives)   ▶ *p. 49* • *GF 8a–b (p. 132)*

Compare the animals. Write sentences with ... than ...

1   (big)   *A hedgehog is bigger than a hamster.*

2   (boring)

3   (pretty)

4   (interesting)

5   (scary)

4017

Did you know?

A hippo can run faster than a man.

○ **18 WORDS   Animals**   ▶ *p. 49*

a) *Find the animal names. Tick (✓) the letters, then write the name and match it with a picture.*

1 ✓b̶ k ✓e̶ ✓a̶ a n ✓r̶ g   _____ bear

2 a m o r n k o e y   _____

3 o l i c o r n o   _____

4 h c i p o p d o i   _____

5 e l e l p h e a c n a t   _____

6 r m h e i l n o   _____

b) *With the extra letters in a) 1–6, find and write the names of three more animals.*

4018

What can you do now?

1 What is it?

1 1 a_____

2 2 _____

3 3 _____

4 4 _____

5 5 _____

6 6 _____

4101

2 What will the weather be like?

Look at the picture. Complete with 'll (will) and won't.

1 In England it _____ be sunny and it _____ rain.

4102 2 In Scotland it _____ rain, but it _____ be cold.

14° Scotland

19° England

3 What will happen if ...?

Complete with the simple present or with 'll (will) ... or won't ...

1 If I _____ (find) a hedgehog baby, I _____ (have to) give it water.

2 It _____ (get ill) if I _____ (give) it milk.

4103 3 If I _____ (not keep) it warm, it _____ (not survive).

4 Describe the pictures.

How? Use adverb forms of:

| careful | fast | hard | angry |

1 Dan is running _____ .

2 Sophie is riding her bike _____ .

3 Ananda is working _____ .

4104 4 Mr Kingsley is shouting _____ .

1

2

4

3

20 points

● **Now you**

In your exercise book, write at least five sentences about your future with 'll (will) and won't.
Ideas: live in Germany/on the moon/under the sea, have a good job, have a car/plane, speak very good English

4105
4106

Unit 4 A weekend in Wales

1 WORDS Town and country ▶ *pp. 60–61*

Find the mistakes in the lists. Mark the wrong words and write them in the correct list.

In town

~~valley~~	*traffic*
forest	
supermarket	
field	
hill	
farm	
museum	
shopping centre	
animals	

In the country

sheep	*valley*
~~traffic~~	
station	
cow	
factory	
cinema	
horse	
DVD shop	
park	
zoo	

4201

2 LISTENING Last weekend ▶ *pp. 60–61* 🎧 11

*Tim and Florian are talking about what they did at the weekend. First, listen to the dialogue. Which **town** words do you hear? Which **country** words do you hear? Listen again and make two lists.*

Town words

station

Country words

farm

4202

3 Where and when (Word order: place before time) ▸ p. 62 • GF 12b (p. 138)

Where will they be on Saturday?

1 Tim – in bed

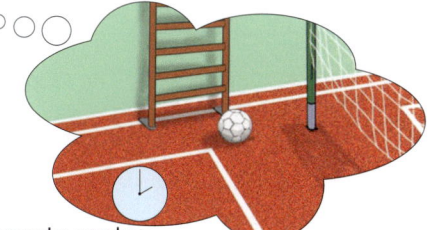

4 Becky – at the sports centre

2 Florian – at the bike shop

5 Becky and Tim – at a party

3 Becky and Lucy – at the shopping centre

 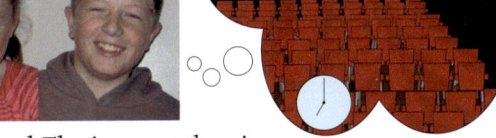

6 Lucy and Florian – at the cinema

1 Tim *will be in bed at nine o'clock.*

2 Florian _____.

3 Becky and Lucy _____.

4 Becky _____.

5 Becky and Tim _____.

4303 6 Lucy and Florian _____.

And I'll be on the best sofa all day …

Now you

Where will you, your mother/father/sister/brother/… probably be next week on Monday, on Saturday or on Sunday? Ideas: **at home, at school, at a birthday party, in town, at a friend's house**
Write at least three sentences.

I'll be at school on Monday.

_____

_____

_____

4 STUDY SKILLS   Topic sentence   ▶ *p. 62 • SF (p. 123)*

Jo is writing an essay about Wales, but he has got a computer virus¹. His sentences are in the wrong order.
Mark the topic sentence in each paragraph and write Jo's sentences in the correct order.

1 Lots of people visit the country every year too. <mark>Wales is only a small country.</mark> About three million people live there.

2 Over 320,000 people live there. There are lots of interesting museums and a castle in the city centre. Cardiff is the biggest city in Wales, with the most people.

3 It's got mountains, valleys and beaches. Wales is a beautiful country too. You can climb the mountains, ride your bike through the valleys or swim in the sea.

4 It's 1,190 metres. Don't go up it if you don't like walking. Snowdon is the biggest mountain in England and Wales.

1 Wales is only a small country. About _____

_____

_____

2 _____

_____

_____

3 _____

_____

_____

4 _____

_____

_____

Did you know?

A village in Wales has a place name with 58 letters. Look!

'Llanfairpwllgwyngyll-gogerychwyrndrobwll Llantysiliogogogoch.'²

But people just say 'Llanfair PG'!

I can say it.
I can say it. Can you?

¹ virus [ˈvaɪrəs]
² You can hear the name at: www.EnglishG.de. Write this web-code: EG21WB44.

Activity page 1

Words in groups   Unit 2

- *Colour the picture cards and cut them out. Then cut out the word cards.*
- *Put the picture cards and the word cards in 3 groups.*
- *On a piece of A4 paper or card, make 3 lists.*
- *Write a group word at the top of each list.*
- *Glue the pictures in the correct lists and glue the correct word cards next to the pictures.*
- *On the empty cards draw 3 more pictures and write 3 more words, one for each list.*

trousers	skirt	ice cream	baseball cap
sweets	cinema tickets	chips	comics
CDs and DVDs	trainers	crisps	magazines

Activity page 2

A puzzle   Unit 4

- *Find the right verb forms.*
- *Cut out the cards in box 2 and complete box 1.*

box 1

go			take		
do			eat		
sing			wear		
give			choose		

✂

ate	done	gone	sung
sang	did	taken	took
wore	eaten	worn	went
chosen	gave	chose	given

box 2

Activity page 3

Memory game: town and country Unit 6

- *Cut out the word cards and the pictures.*
- *Put the cards on the table, so that you can't see the words and the pictures.*
- *Take two cards and match the correct picture and the word card. Go on!*
- *You can play this game with a partner.*

	forest		**river**	
ice rink		**factory**		**market**
	**pub**		**hills**	
valley		**fields**		**supermarket**
	**department store**		**police station**	
railway		**traffic**		**post office**

Activity page 4

A Valentine's Day[1] card

- *Cut out the Valentine's Day card and cut out the three sides of the little window.*
- *Cut out the picture of the bear. Put glue on the sides.*
- *Glue the picture of the bear in the window.*
- *Cut out 'Happy Valentine's Day'. Put the words at the top of the card.*
- *Colour the card.*

[1] *Valentine's Day* [ˈvæləntaɪnz deɪ] *Valentinstag*

5 Dan has called his dad (Present perfect: regular verbs) ▶ *p. 63* • *GF 14a–b (pp. 139–140)*

Find and mark the regular verbs. Choose the correct verb and use it in the present perfect to write a sentence under each picture. Then match and add a sentence from the box.

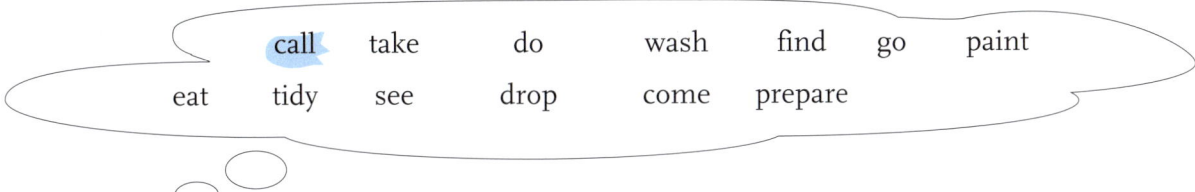

call   take   do   wash   find   go   paint
eat   tidy   see   drop   come   prepare

It smells great. • *Now Mr Shaw is happy.* • Now they are wet too. • Poor Barnabas! •
Now his mum will be happy. • Now their jeans are red and green too.

1 Dan – dad

Dan has called his dad.

Now Mr Shaw is happy.

_____

2 Grandma – some Welsh soup

_____

_____

_____

3 Tim and Florian – their skateboards

_____

_____

_____

4 Tim – his ice cream

_____

_____

_____

5 Sophie and Toby – Sheeba

_____

_____

_____

6 Tim – his room

_____

_____

_____

6 Find the forms (Past participles: irregular verbs)   ▶ *p. 63* • *GF 14a–b (pp. 139–140)*

Find the missing past participles in the snake and complete the lists.

Wait**been**eatencleandonewalkfoundgonetrymadecometakenseen

be – was – *been* _____   see – saw – _____   take – took – _____

go – went – _____   find – found – _____   do – did – _____

4606 eat – ate – _____   make – made – _____   come – came – _____

7 Monday morning at the Muddles' (Present perfect: already, not … yet)   ▶ *p. 63* • *GF 15 (p. 141)*

What have the Muddles already done? What haven't they done yet? Write a sentence under each picture.
*Use the present perfect with **already** or **not … yet**.*

have a shower   do his homework   take out the rubbish

make their beds   go to school   eat their breakfast

1 Max *has already had a shower.* _____   2 Molly and Micky *haven't made their beds yet.* _____

3 Mr Muddles _____   4 Maggie and Minnie _____

_____.   _____.

5 Molly and Micky _____   6 Max _____

4607   _____.   _____.

Now you

What have you already done today? What haven't you done yet?
Write at least four sentences in your exercise book.

I've already had lunch. I haven't phoned my friends yet.

8 Jack has just … (Present perfect: just) ▸ *p. 63* • *GF 15 (p. 141)*

What have they just done? Complete the sentences. Use a verb from the list in the present perfect and just*.*

| clean | eat | make | pack | see |

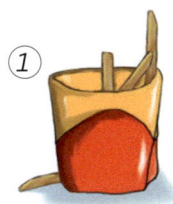    

1   Jack isn't hungry. *He has just eaten some chips.*

2   Ananda is ready for the hockey match. She _____ .

3   It smells good in the kitchen. Sophie _____ .

4   Emily and her friend are nervous. They _____ .

4708   5   The Thompsons are planning a trip. Grandpa _____ .

9 WORDS Body words ▸ *p. 64*

a) Write the answers in the puzzle.

1   You smell with this.

2   If you eat too much, this can hurt.

3   You have ten of these.

4   You talk and eat with this.

5   We've got two arms and two…

6   You think with this.

7   This starts with a 'k' – but you don't hear it.

4709   8   An elephant has very big ones.

1								_ _ _ _			
2											
3							_ _ _ s		
4							_ _ _ _		
5							_ _ _ s	
6						_ _ _			
7							_ _ _ _		
8							_ _ s		

b) What's the word in the green boxes?

Tim has played football with his friends.

▸ Now his _____ hurts.

*c) Tim tells his mum. Write a short dialogue in your exercise book.
Use ideas from your student's book, p. 64.*

Mum: What's the matter, Tim?

Tim: I …

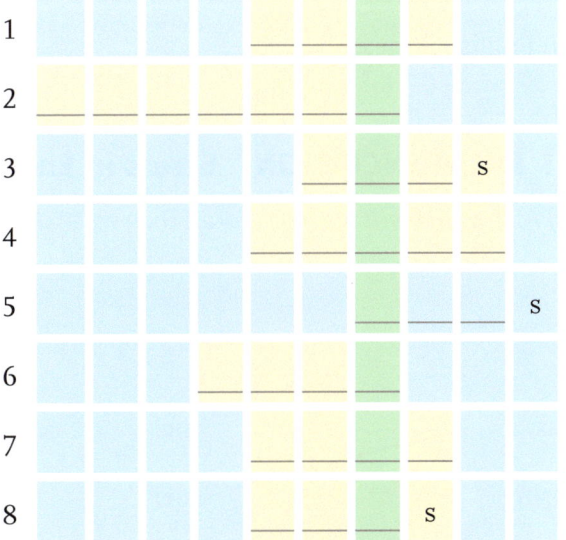

Just for fun

Hello, Ed. What's the matter with you? Ah. You can't talk. I know! You have a sore throat.

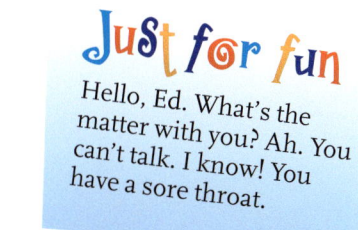

10 WORDS   Find the message   ▸ *p. 64*

a) *Label the pictures.*

f a c t o r y   (3)

(1)

(2)

(3)

(3)

(2)

(2)

(4)

(7)

(4)

(3)

(3)

b)   **Extra**   *Find the letters in the green boxes, then write the message.*

The message is   C _____ !

In English it means   _____ !

11 PRONUNCIATION   Stress in English and German (Betonung)   ▸ *p. 64* 🎧 12

a) *Match and write correct words. Then write the German words. Listen to the words and mark the stress.*

ca	nic
kang	mel
temper	phant
pic	aroo
gar	over
pull	age
acc	ature
ele	ent

camel   Kamel

_____   _____

_____   _____

_____   _____

_____   _____

_____   _____

_____   _____

_____   _____

b) *One word has the same stress in English and German. Draw a* *next to it.*

12 Have they ever …? (Present perfect: questions with ever) ▸ p. 65 • GF 14c, 15 (pp. 140–141)

Look at the pictures and write questions. Then write short answers.
Use: been, seen, found, played, eaten

Q: <u>Has Ananda ever been to</u> New York?

A: Yes, _____ .

Q: Has _____ ?

A: _____

Q: Have the twins _____ ?

A: _____

> No, thank you.

Q: _____

A: _____

Q: _____

4912 A: _____

Q: _____ Toby and Emily _____ ?

A: _____

13 REVISION The football match (Conditional sentences 1) ▸ p. 65 • GF 10 (p. 135)

Fill in the correct forms.

Dan   It's the big match on Saturday. If Ed's knee still <u>hurts</u> (hurt), he
<u>won't play</u> (not play) in the team. That will be terrible.

Jo   Right. If he _____ (not feel) better, his mum _____ (say)
he can't play.

Dan   If he _____ (not play), who _____ (play) for him? Sam?

Jo   Yes, Sam. But he isn't as good as Ed. If our team _____ (play) badly,
Mr Kingsley _____ (not be) very happy.

Dan   I know. If we _____ (lose) another match, we _____ (not be)
the champions this year.

Jo   Right. If we _____ (not win), the team _____ (be) really sad.
4913   And if I _____ (play) badly, Dad _____ (not buy) me a new football.

14 READING ...   ▸ *p. 65*

a) Read the story.

Three years ago the Baxters visited a castle in Wales. Becky can remember the visit very well ...
'It was a great visit,' said Tim. 'It was very funny too!' '*You* thought it was funny. But it was horrible for me,' said Becky. Lucy wanted to know why the visit was so horrible.
'Well,' said Tim. 'When we looked round the castle, I stayed with Mum and Dad, but Becky wanted to explore alone.'
'Be quiet!' said Becky angrily. 'I can tell Lucy the story.'
'Is it exciting?' asked Lucy with big eyes.
'Go on. Tell me about it!'
'Well, you see,' said Becky 'there was a tower, and in the tower I went up some stairs. I found a little door. Of course I wanted to know what was behind it, so I opened it and went inside. But it was windy, and – bang! The door closed behind me. I was alone in the dark. I shouted and shouted. I shouted so loudly that I had a sore throat, but nobody came. Then suddenly I heard a noise behind me. Something moved. I felt really scared.'
'Wow! Well, go on, what was it? Something horrible?' Lucy wanted to know. 'How exciting!'
'I don't know. It was very dark in the room – and cold too. Just awful,' said Becky.

'Well, the castle is very old, and I think maybe there were a few very old dead bodies in there. Or maybe there was a cold, dangerous animal – a crocodile, a big snake or ...,' said Tim.
'You're mad, Tim. I'm sure it was just a mouse,' Lucy went on. 'Well, what happened then?'
'Now it's my turn,' said Tim. 'Listen carefully. This is the best part of the story. Well, we didn't know where Becky was. But Mum and Dad didn't worry because Becky is always careful. But when we went in the tower, I heard a noise. I thought it was a girl's voice, so I explored ...'

5014

b) Find the best title for the story:

| A | A great castle | | B | A scary story | | C | A nice day out |

c) What's right? Tick (✔) A, B or C.

1 The Baxters visited a castle in ...	A	Wales.	B	England.	C	Scotland.
2 They went there ...	A	last year.	B	three years ago.	C	two years ago.
3 Becky thought the visit was ...	A	funny.	B	exciting.	C	horrible.
4 Lucy thought the story was ...	A	boring.	B	exciting.	C	sad.
5 Becky was in the tower ...	A	alone.	B	with her parents.	C	with Tim.
6 In the room it was ...	A	dark and hot.	B	hot and wet.	C	cold and dark.

15 WRITING   The end of the story   ▶ p. 65 • SF (p. 123)

Read the story in exercise 14 again and complete it. Here are some words, but you can use your own ideas.
Write eight sentences or more.

> open • find • cry • happy • brother • laugh • hero • save Becky's life • mouse

Tim went on, 'And then I saw the door. I _____

_____

_____

_____

_____

_____

_____

16 WORDS   My first is in ...   ▶ p. 65

a) What am I?

1	My first is in	page	but not in	cage	. ___p___
2	My second is in	ate	but not in	pet	. _____
3	My third is in	tree	but not in	tea	. _____
4	My fourth is in	hear	but not in	here	. _____
5	My fifth is in	mad	but not in	dad	. _____
6	My sixth is in	men	but not in	man	. _____
7	My seventh is in	date	but not in	late	. _____
8	My eighth is in	said	but not in	sad	. _____
9	And my last is in	chair	but not in	hair	. _____

My first
is in 'clever' but
not in ...

b) What's my name? It rhymes with **win**. If you know, complete the sentence.

My name is _____ and I'm a _____ .

17 WORDS   Have you ever …? ▶ *p. 65*

a) Find the missing word in the blue box, write it down and then cross it out in the blue box.

1 Have you … been to Australia? – No, never.   *ever* _____

2 Look, I've … a new CD.   _____

3 If you feel very hot, maybe you have a …   _____

4 I've got a … throat. It really hurts.   _____

5 I don't feel well. I think I've got a …   _____

6 Tim hasn't … Barnabas. He's hungry.   _____

7 If you don't clean your teeth, you'll get a …   _____

> TEMPERATUREWETOOTHACHELS~~EVER~~H
> BOUGHTGFEDRASORENNCOLDY

5217 *b) Which letters are still in the blue box? Make two words.* Answer: _____

18 WORDS   Computer words ▶ *p. 65*

Find and write the computer words.

s	u	r	f	d	m	l	f	p
o	c	v	c	o	p	y	g	r
f	l	v	s	w	b	n	w	i
t	i	a	e	n	t	e	r	n
w	c	e	n	l	r	-	h	t
a	k	u	d	o	d	m	k	☺
r	☺	c	h	a	t	a	j	o
e	o	p	t	d	p	i	o	u
i	n	s	t	a	l	l	p	t

▶ *surf* _____

_____

_____

_____

▼ *software* _____

_____

_____

_____

_____

Now you

*Write at least five sentences about your computer in your exercise book. Use words from exercise **18**.*

I like to surf on my computer. I can write …

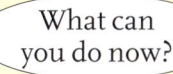

What can you do now?

1 What's in the picture?

1 _____
2 _____
3 _____
4 _____
5 _____
6 _____

5301

2 Write correct sentences.

1 I'll – at five-thirty – be – at the station.

_____
_____

2 We – till six – in the DVD shop – were.

_____
_____

5302

3 What have they done?

Use the present perfect of **drop**, **find**, **make**, **pack** *and complete the sentences.*

1 Ananda _____.

2 Jo _____.

3 The Thompsons _____.

4 Emma _____.

5303

4 Complete the words.

Mum   Tim, what's the m _____? Are you feeling i _____?

Tim   Yes, my throat h _____ and I have a t _____. And my head. I have a
      h _____ too. And my legs hurt when I m _____. I can't go to school today.

5304   Mum   Really? But the French test is today…

18 points

● Now you

*In your exercise book, write three or four short paragraphs about your country. Start each paragraph with a topic sentence. You can use ideas from Jo's essay in exercise **4** (workbook, p. 44) or look at English websites about Germany for ideas. For example, try www.germany-tourism.de.*

5305
5306

Jetzt kann ich ...   Sehr gut! | OK | Verbessern!

HÖREN: Ich kann ...

... die Anweisungen, Fragen und Erklärungen im Unterricht verstehen. ☐ ☐ ☐

... den Sinn einfacher Geschichten und Lieder verstehen. ☐ ☐ ☐

... eine längere Geschichte verstehen, auch wenn mir nicht alle Wörter bekannt sind. ☐ ☐ ☐

... verschiedene Akzente erkennen. ☐ ☐ ☐

... die Vokabeln der Units 3 und 4 verstehen. ☐ ☐ ☐

SPRECHEN: Ich kann ...

... zu einem bestimmten Thema ein paar zusammenhängende Sätze frei sprechen, auch wenn ich kleine Fehler mache. ☐ ☐ ☐

... die Wörter der Units 3 und 4 richtig aussprechen und anwenden. ☐ ☐ ☐

... über Tiere im Wald und ihre Gewohnheiten sprechen. ☐ ☐ ☐

... sagen, was mir wehtut und andere fragen, was ihnen gesundheitlich fehlt. ☐ ☐ ☐

... die Konsonantenlaute [f], [v] und [w] voneinander unterscheiden und richtig aussprechen. ☐ ☐ ☐

LESEN: Ich kann ...

... eine Postkarte oder einen kurzen Brief auf Englisch lesen und verstehen. ☐ ☐ ☐

... die längeren Erzähltexte und Dialoge der Units 3 und 4 lesen und verstehen. ☐ ☐ ☐

... die längeren Erzähltexte und Dialoge der Units 3 und 4 ohne Probleme laut vorlesen. ☐ ☐ ☐

... kurze Sachtexte lesen und verstehen. ☐ ☐ ☐

... Texte über Themen des Alltags lesen und verstehen, auch wenn mir nicht alle Wörter bekannt sind. ☐ ☐ ☐

SCHREIBEN: Ich kann ...

... kurze und einfache E-Mails, Briefe oder Postkarten schreiben. ☐ ☐ ☐

... einfache Fragen zu den Texten der Units 3 und 4 schriftlich beantworten. ☐ ☐ ☐

... meine Sätze mit *time phrases* wie *first, then, after that, a few minutes later* miteinander verbinden. Dadurch klingen meine Texte interessanter. ☐ ☐ ☐

... meine Sätze mit *linking words* (z.B. *because, so, but*) miteinander verbinden, damit meine Texte flüssiger klingen. ☐ ☐ ☐

... die Wörter der Units 3 und 4 richtig schreiben. ☐ ☐ ☐

LAND UND LEUTE: Ich ...

... weiß etwas über den britischen Tierverein RSPCA. ☐ ☐ ☐

... habe etwas über Wales und über die walisische Sprache gelernt. ☐ ☐ ☐

Jetzt kann ich ...   Sehr gut!   OK   Verbessern!

GRAMMATIKVERSTÄNDNIS: Ich kann ...

... mit *will/won't* + Infinitiv (*will-future*) über die Zukunft sprechen und Vorhersagen machen (z.B. *I'll be 14 next year*). ⃞ ⃞ ⃞

... mit einem *Conditional sentence* (*type 1*) ausdrücken, was unter bestimmten Bedingungen geschehen wird (z.B. *If you give a hedgehog water, it'll be happy*). ⃞ ⃞ ⃞

... mit Adverbien der Art und Weise beschreiben, wie jemand etwas macht oder sagt. Adverbien bilde ich, indem ich *-ly* an das Adjektiv anhänge (z.B. *A hedgehog walks slowly*). Ich kenne auch die unregelmäßigen Adverbformen (z.B. *I work well/hard/fast*). ⃞ ⃞ ⃞

... die Verbformen des *present perfect* erkennen und richtig bilden (z.B. *I have looked/been, he/she has looked/been*). ⃞ ⃞ ⃞

... mit dem *present perfect* ausdrücken, was ich oder andere irgendwann in der Vergangenheit gemacht haben (z.B. *Jo has bought a new DVD*). ⃞ ⃞ ⃞

VOKABELVERSTÄNDNIS: Ich kann ...

... die Namen einiger Wild- und Zootiere (z.B. *squirrel, bear, lion*) richtig verwenden. ⃞ ⃞ ⃞

... Wörter für Stadt und Land (z.B. *valley, field, forest, traffic*) richtig verwenden. ⃞ ⃞ ⃞

... Wörter für Körperteile (z.B. *shoulder, stomach, ear, throat*) richtig verwenden. ⃞ ⃞ ⃞

... Wörter für einige Krankheiten (z.B. *a cold, a toothache*) richtig verwenden. ⃞ ⃞ ⃞

SKILLS – LERNEN UND ARBEITEN: Ich ...

... kann in meinem Dictionary ein Wort ohne Probleme nachschlagen. ⃞ ⃞ ⃞

... kann während des Hörens eines Hörtextes kurze Notizen dazu machen. ⃞ ⃞ ⃞

... kann in einem langen Text nach Schlüsselwörtern suchen, um gezielte Informationen schnell zu finden. Im Englischen nennt man dies *scanning*. ⃞ ⃞ ⃞

... weiß, dass ich in meinem Text einen Absatz mit einem *topic sentence* anfangen muss, der aussagt, worum es in dem Absatz geht. ⃞ ⃞ ⃞

WAS ICH FÜR MEIN ENGLISCHLERNEN GETAN HABE: Ich habe ...   häufig   manchmal   nie

... ausprobiert, mit welchen Lern- und Arbeitstechniken ich am besten lernen und arbeiten kann. ⃞ ⃞ ⃞

... die Aufgaben im Grammar File in meinem Buch bearbeitet. ⃞ ⃞ ⃞

... die Aufgaben im Skills File in meinem Buch bearbeitet. ⃞ ⃞ ⃞

WIE ICH MICH VERBESSERN KÖNNTE: Ich könnte ...

... am Unterricht aktiver teilnehmen. ⃞

... neue und auch alte Vokabeln regelmäßig wiederholen. ⃞

... nach jedem neuen Skills-Abschnitt in meinem Buch den dazugehörigen Abschnitt im Skills File aufmerksam lesen. ⃞

... versuchen, bekannte Texte aus meinem Buch schriftlich und auch mündlich nachzuerzählen. ⃞

... Übungen aus früheren Units in meinem Buch/Workbook noch einmal durcharbeiten. ⃞

... häufiger mit meinen Hörtexten arbeiten. ⃞

Unit 5 Teamwork

1 WORDS Let's play the Bristol Game! ▶ pp. 76–77

a) First, write the answers in the boxes.

1 You need it to play. It can be red, yellow, blue or green.

2 It has six numbers on it.

3 Sometimes you have to move …

4 Sometimes you have to miss a …

5 If you get to number 50 first, you …

6 The game is about this city.

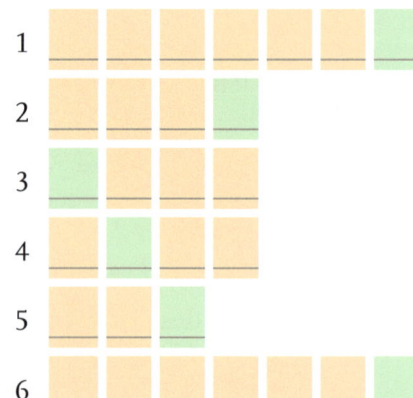

b) Now make the name of a famous person from the letters in the green boxes.

5601 The name is _____ .

2 WORDS About Bristol ▶ pp. 76–77

Complete with the missing words from the boxes. Write them correctly.

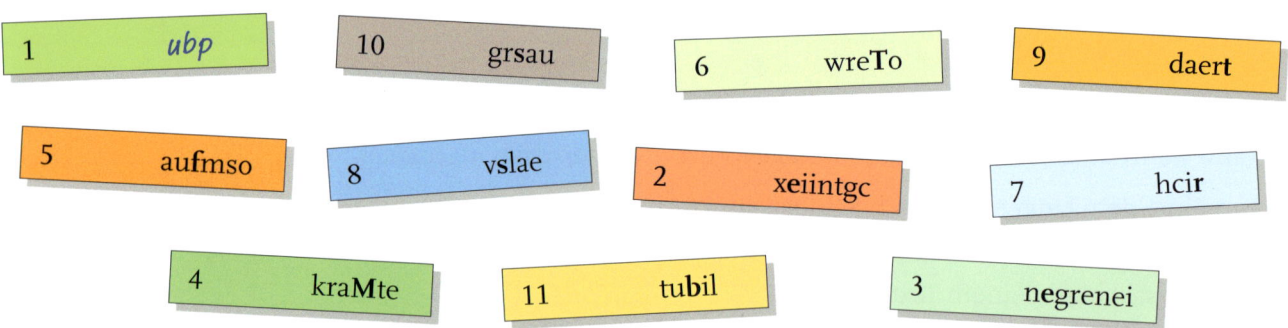

The Llandoger Trow is an old Bristol (1) *pub* .

Explore-at-Bristol is an (2)_____ science museum.

Brunel was a famous (3)_____ .

At St Nicholas (4)_____ you can get a healthy snack.

You can walk over the River Avon on the (5)_____ Clifton Suspension Bridge.

You can climb the famous Cabot (6)_____ too.

Bristol got (7)_____ from the (8)_____ (9)_____ .

5602 A family in the (10)_____ trade (11)_____ the Georgian House in 1791.

3 PRONUNCIATION   Silent letters   ▶ p. 78 🎧 13

Listen to the words and find the silent letters. Mark them in red. How many are there?

Shhhhhh!
L i s t̶e n!

b u s i n e s s	w o u l d	i s l a n d
h a l f	h o u r	c a s t l e
c l i m b	s w i m	a n s w e r W e d n e s d a y

5703

4 WORDS   Pairs   ▶ p. 78

a) *Which words go together? Find and write pairs.*

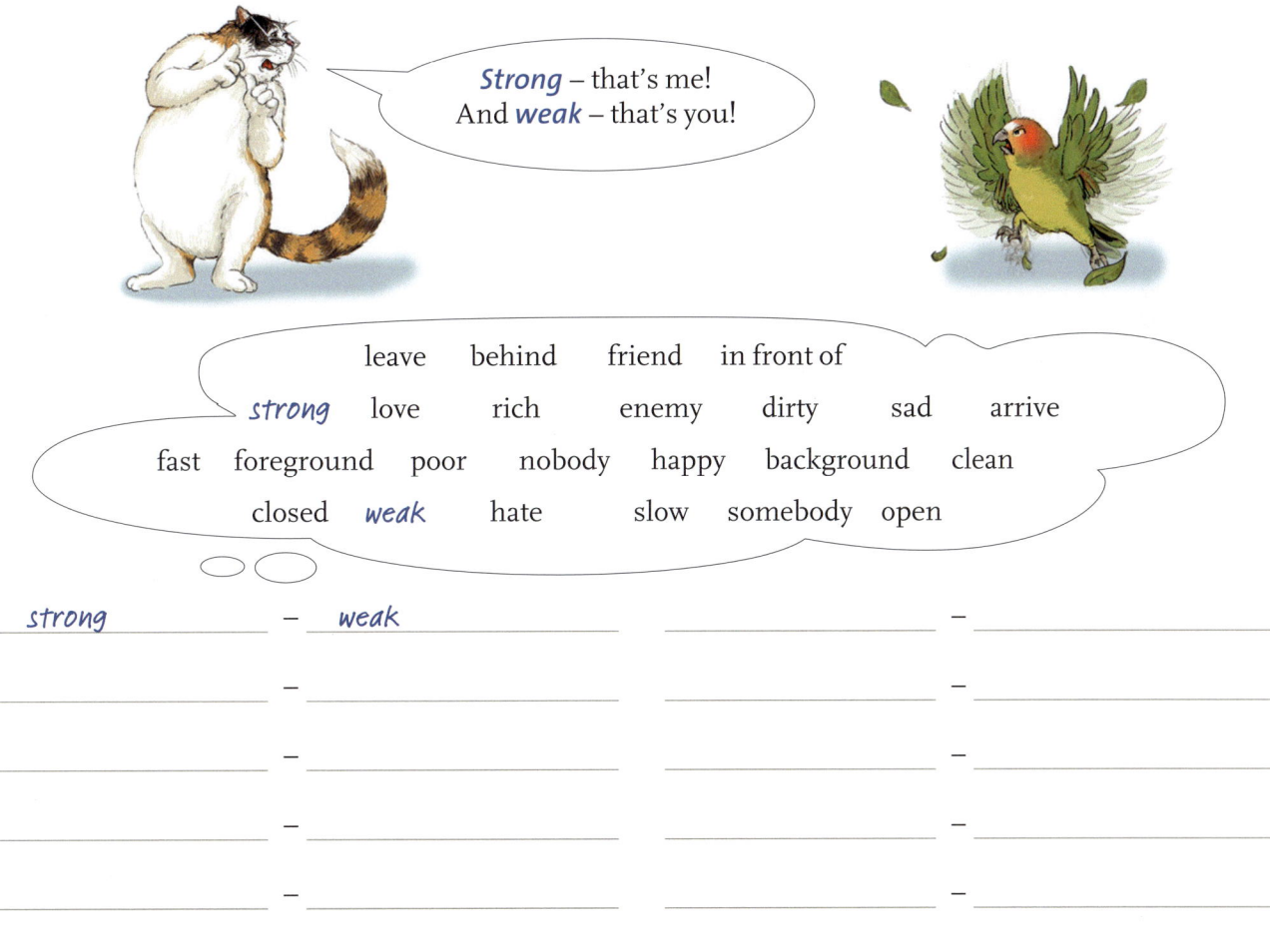

Strong – that's me!
And *weak* – that's you!

leave   behind   friend   in front of
strong   love   rich   enemy   dirty   sad   arrive
fast   foreground   poor   nobody   happy   background   clean
closed   *weak*   hate   slow   somebody   open

strong ___ – ___ weak ___   ___ – ___

___ – ___   ___ – ___

___ – ___   ___ – ___

___ – ___   ___ – ___

___ – ___   ___ – ___

5704

___ – ___

b) *Choose five pairs and use them in five sentences. Write in your exercise book.*

My brother <u>loves</u> school, but he <u>hates</u> homework.

5 Who's who? (Relative clauses)   ▶ p. 78 • GF 17a (p. 142)

Write sentences about the Bristol kids with **girl** or **boy** and **who**.

 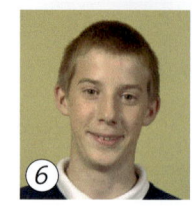

has a dog called Scruffy
is in the school Dance Club
tried to help Jody in Cornwall
helps her parents in their shop
loves football
hates sport

1 Ananda *is the girl who helps her parents in their shop.* _____

2 Lesley _____ .

3 Jack _____ .

4 Jo _____ .

5 Sophie _____ .

5805 6 Dan _____ .

6 Who or what are they? (Relative clauses)   ▶ p. 78 • GF 17a (p. 142)

Complete the sentences with **who** or **which** and information from the box.

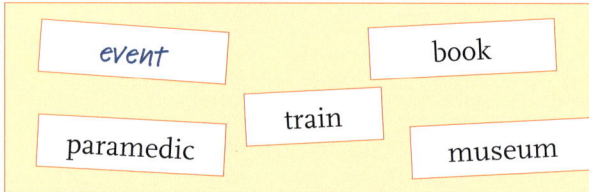

event	book	lives near the Thompsons

event   book   train   paramedic   museum

lives near the Thompsons
describes the life of three children and a horse
travels through the Brecon Beacons
begins in August
teaches visitors lots about science

1 The Balloon Fiesta is *an event which begins in August.* _____

2 Bryn is _____ .

3 Explore-at-Bristol is _____ .

4 The Brecon Mountain Railway is _____ .

5806 5 *No Small Thing* is _____ .

● **Now you**

In your exercise book, describe these
persons and animals with **who** *and* **which**.

Number ... is a person/an animal ...

7 Sarah is the girl whose ... (Relative clauses) ▶ p. 79 • GF 17b (p. 142)

Write sentences with whose.

1 girl – dad lives in New York

2 boy – mum works for the BBC

3 twins – parents want to move to Australia

4 brothers – family has a café

5 boy – brother plays in our school football team

6 girl – sister sings in our school band

1 Sarah *is the girl whose dad lives in New York.*

2 Peter _____ .

3 Ann and Sally *are* _____ .

4 Rob and Leo _____ .

5 Mike _____ .

5907

6 Trish _____ .

8 STUDY SKILLS   Marking up a text ▶ p. 79 • SF (p. 121)

Mark up the text about John Cabot. Which information in each paragraph is the most important? Think about ...

1 when Cabot was young.
2 when he was a man.
3 what made him famous.
4 how people can remember him today.

Who was John Cabot?

He was born in Genoa, Italy in 1450, and his name was really Giovanni Caboto.
When John was young, his father told him stories about countries far away, and about Marco Polo. John wanted to be a sailor[1] and an explorer too. It was his dream to explore the world in a ship.

When John was a man, he moved with his family to Bristol, where there were many sailors. He planned to find a new sea route[2] to the west. Some rich men in Bristol found his plans very interesting and they gave him money for a ship. He built a small but fast ship with the name 'Matthew'[3].

Cabot left from Bristol with his ship and 18 men in 1497. He wanted to find new land in the west. Six weeks later he found Newfoundland in Canada. When he came back to England, King Henry VII gave him some money. A year later Cabot left Bristol again for Newfoundland, now with five ships and 300 men. But this time he did not come back. Nobody heard of him again.

400 years later in 1897, the people of Bristol built the Cabot Tower to remember John Cabot, their 'Bristol explorer'. The red tower is 30 metres. You can climb to the top, and on a sunny day you have a beautiful view of the city.
There is also a Cabot Tower in St John's, Newfoundland, where John Cabot first landed.

[1]sailor ['seɪlə] *Seemann*   [2]route [ruːt] *Route*   [3]Matthew ['mæθjuː]

9 At the juice bar ▶ p. 80

Read p. 80 in your student's book again. Write a dialogue between an assistant and Becky at the juice bar.
Use the words from the box or your own ideas.

> delicious · flavour · healthy · *help* · small one · smoothie · strawberry

Assistant   Hello. How can I _help_ you?

Becky   I'd like _____.

Assistant   _____

Becky   _____

Assistant   _____

6009 Becky   _____

10 It's my turn, isn't it? (Question tags) ▶ p. 80 · GF 18 (p. 143)

What do they say? Choose the correct question tag and complete the speech bubbles.

> wasn't it?   is it?   was it?   is she?   aren't you?   aren't they?   *isn't it?*

1 Now it's my turn, *isn't it* ?

2 No, Lucy! It was your turn last time, _____ ?

3 Becky, you're yellow, _____ ? Tim, that's Becky's counter!

4 Hey! It wasn't a six, _____ ? It was a four!

5 Hey! It isn't Lucy's turn, _____ ?

6 Oh, no! Lucy isn't the winner again, _____ ? She always wins.

7 That isn't fair! The winners are always the worst players, _____ ?

6110

11 We've got all the answers, haven't we? (Question tags) ▶ p. 80 • GF 18 (p. 143)

Complete the sentences with the right question tags in the right tense.

Jack	We've got all the answers for the quiz now, _haven't we_? Let's check.
	The Balloon Fiesta begins in August, _____?
Jo	Right. And visitors have to look up a lot, _____?
Dan	Right. But you haven't downloaded any photos yet, Jo, _____?
Jo	No, and Ananda hasn't finished the texts yet, _____? But let's check
	all the answers first. Now, Question 2. What do we know about Brunel?
	He's very famous, _____?
Dan	Right. He died in 1859. And in Bristol he built a station, a bridge and a
	ship, _____?
Jack	OK. Now Question 3. The healthy and delicious drinks were at the Big Banana
	juice bar, _____? And I think the smallest drink was Sophie's
	wheatgrass juice, _____? Maybe that was the most interesting too.
	But it wasn't the cheapest, _____? Which drink was the cheapest?
Jo	Oh, dear! I think I know which the cheapest drink was. Mine!
	Because I think I forgot[1] to pay ...

6111

12 LISTENING   Teamwork   ▶ p. 80 🎧 14

a) *Listen carefully to Tim, Becky and Florian. Then tick (✓) the correct boxes.*

	Right	Wrong	Don't know
1 Tim and his friends are going to write a report for school.	☐	☐	☐
2 They have to do interviews with the sports teams.	☐	☐	☐
3 Florian is a good photographer.	☐	☐	☐
4 Tim has got a new camera now.	☐	☐	☐
5 Florian wants to argue.	☐	☐	☐
6 Lucy is going to do an interview with the judo team.	☐	☐	☐
7 Becky is in the junior tennis team.	☐	☐	☐
8 Florian is in the junior basketball team.	☐	☐	☐
9 Tim is going to check all the match results.	☐	☐	☐
10 Becky and Lucy are going to do all the computer work.	☐	☐	☐

6112

● **b)** *Becky isn't happy about Tim's teamwork for the Sports Centre newspaper. Say why not.*
Write two or three sentences in your exercise book.

[1]forgot [fəˈɡɒt] *vergaß*

13 WORDS   Word bridges   ▶ p. 81

How many words can you make from the word bridges? Use the Dictionary in your student's book (pp. 178–199).

calendar, chair, _____

_____

painter, _____

_____

_____

6213

_____

14 STUDY SKILLS   Structuring a text   ▶ p. 81 • SF (p. 123)

Lucy has written a text about the Bristol Balloon Fiesta. Read the text carefully and mark three paragraphs (beginning, middle and end) in three different colours.

Every year in August there's the Bristol Balloon Fiesta, Europe's biggest show of hot-air balloons. It's the most exciting thing to do in Bristol in August. Hundreds of beautiful balloons from different countries meet in Europe – and about 500,000 visitors come to watch. It's great if the weather is good. If it's too windy, the balloons can't fly. But there's more than just balloon flights. There's a full programme of things to do and lots of fun things for kids too. There are live concerts with cool pop groups, games, shows, prizes to win, a food market, camel rides, even a Wild West show. I've been to the Fiesta three times with my parents and friends. It's really cool to watch the balloons and you can take great photos.

15 WRITING An e-mail ▶ p. 81

*Imagine you were at the Bristol Balloon Fiesta too. Write an e-mail to a friend about it. Use words and ideas from Lucy's text in exercise **14**. Don't forget to use **first**, **then**, **after that**, **in the afternoon**, etc.*
Write at least six sentences.

Dear _____

Last weekend I went to the Bristol Balloon Fiesta with some friends. It's the biggest hot-air balloon

show in Europe. I'll tell you about it. First we _____

_____

_____

_____

_____

_____

16 MEDIATION At the juice bar ▶ p. 81 • SF (p. 125)

Florian is with his cousin Heike and his German uncle and aunt in a juice bar. They don't speak much English.
What does Florian say?

Assistant	Hello, how can I help you today? As always we've got our delicious smoothies in different flavours. Our special smoothie today is kiwi and banana. And of course we've got our fruit juices and our fruit salad, as always.
Uncle	Was hat er gesagt? Ich habe nichts verstanden. Der Typ redet zu viel und zu schnell.
Florian	(to uncle): *Er hat tolle Smoothies heute und Säfte auch.* _____
Aunt	Was hat er? Sm… Sm… Was ist das? Frag ihn bitte.
Florian	(to assistant): *My aunt* _____
	_____
Assistant	Oh, well, you make it with fruit and milk or ice cream. Very healthy and delicious.
Florian	(to aunt): *Es wird aus* _____
	_____
Uncle	Heutzutage muss immer alles gesund sein. Nein, danke. Ich nehme eine Cola.
Florian	(to assistant): _____
Aunt	Und ich nehme so einen 'Schmusi'. Erdbeere, wenn sie es haben. Banane geht auch.
Florian	_____
Heike	Gute Idee. Für mich auch.
Florian	OK. Dann nehme ich dasselbe.
	(to assistant): _____

17 WORKING WITH THE TEXT To catch a thief ▶ pp. 88–90

a) *Read pp. 86–88 in your student's book again. Who says what? Match the sentences to the speakers.*

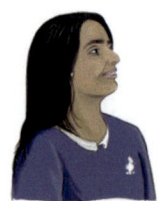

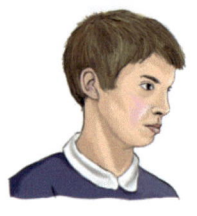

Dan

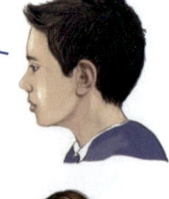

Jo

Who is stealing things from Form 8PK?

Well, it can only be one person.

And I don't think Lesley's a thief!

We have to catch the thief and we need proof.

And I put some money in the purse too: five pounds.

And I suppose you think this somebody is me.

Hello, Mr Smith. What can I do for you?

You really have to look after your things better, you know.

Oh dear. Not one of the SHoCK Team's great cases, eh?

You shouldn't go round and say people have stolen things before you're sure.

b) *Complete with beginnings or ends to make correct sentences.*

1　David's mobile was in the classsroom, but __then it disappeared/somebody took it.__

2　__Jo thought/said__ the thief was Lesley.

3　Jack was angry. He said, _____

4　'And how are we going to get proof?' asked Jo. Jack smiled: _____

5　Sophie said, '_____
_____ that bleeps when you whistle.'

6　'We put the key ring in the purse … _____

7　At the end of break Sophie whispered, _____

8　_____ the bleeps got louder.

9　Mr Smith opened his bag and _____

10　Mr Kingsley said, 'So listen to Mr Smith or _____

c) *Was Jo fair to Lesley? Why or why not? Explain. Write a few sentences in your exercise book.*

I think Jo was/wasn't …

What can you do now?

1 What's the opposite¹?

1 open   – _____

2 rich   – _____

3 arrive – _____

4 friendly – _____

5 possible – _____

6 agree   – _____

6501

2 Complete the sentences.

*Choose **who**, **which** or **whose** and the right information from the boxes.*

takes place in a park in August.

invented Wallace and Gromit.

found Newfoundland.

statue stands in Bristol?

1 Cabot was the explorer _____

2 Who is the famous engineer _____

3 Nick Park is the man _____

4 The Bristol Balloon Fiesta is an event _____

3 Complete the words.

Assistant   Hi. What can I g_____ you?

Tim   I'd like a s_____, please.

A_____   What f_____ would you like?

     Today we've got banana, strawberry, orange and kiwi too.

6503   They're all d_____ and very h_____.

4 Circle the correct question tag.

Tim   This is a cool juice bar,   isn't it? / is it?

Lucy   Yes, and the people are friendly,   isn't it? / aren't they?

Tim   And it wasn't too expensive,   wasn't it? / was it?

6504 *Lucy*   And the smoothies were great,   weren't they? / were they?

20 points

● **Now you**

6505 *Do you like teamwork in projects? How many times have you done teamwork with classmates or friends?*

6506 *Write at least five sentences about teamwork in your exercise book.*

¹ opposite [ˈɒpəzɪt] *Gegenteil*

Unit 6 A trip to Bath

1 WORDS   Lists and more   ▸ pp. 94–95

a) *Write the words in the correct lists.*

Roman · room · jump · round · relax · stone · enjoy · cold · wall · have a bath ·
hot · have a sauna · statue · feel · warm · dark · towel · pool

ADJECTIVES	NOUNS	VERBS
Roman	room	jump
_____	_____	_____
_____	_____	_____
_____	_____	_____
_____	_____	_____

6601

b) *Look at the pictures. What's happening? Use the mosaic pieces to make sentences to describe the pictures.*

1

2

is		the		relaxing	
	pool		Roman		hot
the		in		men	
	are		boy		Roman
into		jumping		cold	
					room

1 A *Roman boy* _____ .

6602 2 Two _____ .

2 WORDS Word building ▸ p. 96

a) Which pairs go together? Find, colour and write the pairs.

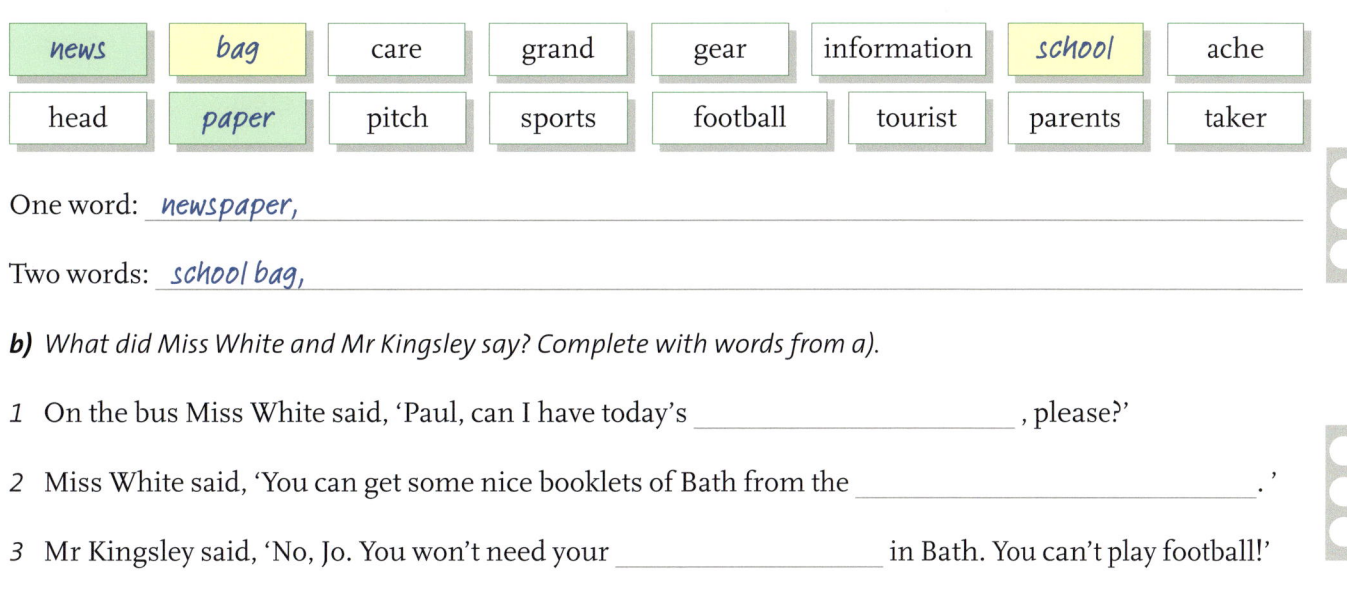

news	bag	care	grand	gear	information	school	ache
head	paper	pitch	sports	football	tourist	parents	taker

One word: _newspaper,_

Two words: _school bag,_

b) What did Miss White and Mr Kingsley say? Complete with words from a).

1 On the bus Miss White said, 'Paul, can I have today's _____ , please?'

2 Miss White said, 'You can get some nice booklets of Bath from the _____ .'

6702 3 Mr Kingsley said, 'No, Jo. You won't need your _____ in Bath. You can't play football!'

3 Extra The school trip (Relative clauses: contact clauses) ▸ p. 96 • GF 19 (p. 144)

a) Find six sentences where you don't need a relative pronoun. Write them again as contact clauses.
You need the letters in brackets ( ) in b).

> The students are riding along the railway path which goes to Warmley (s). It's the nicest bike ride that
> Mr Kingsley knows (m). From Warmley they are going to take the bus that goes to Bath (h). Bath is one
> of the nicest cities that Miss White knows (u). Miss White is the other teacher who is going on the trip
> (o). First they are going to visit the famous Baths which the Romans built (s). Lesley is the girl who Jo
> doesn't like very much (e). Jack is the boy who is nice to Lesley (p). Jack is the boy who Lesley likes a lot
> (u). Lesley is the only student who has never been to Bath (s). Designing clothes is something that
> Lesley wants to do one day (m).

1 _It's the nicest bike ride Mr Kingsley knows._ _____ _m_

2 _____ _____

3 _____ _____

4 _____ _____

5 _____ _____

6 _____ _____

b) Now write down the letters in brackets ( ) after the six sentences. If your answers are correct, the new word
tells you where the students are going in the afternoon. Complete this sentence:

▸ In the afternoon the students and their teachers are going to visit a _____ .

4 STUDY SKILLS   Having a conversation   ▶ p. 96 • SF (p. 122)

Florian is talking to Mrs Baxter. Add phrases to make the dialogue more friendly.
Choose from the box or use your own ideas.

> Everything is fine. • You'll like it. • And how are you? • thanks (2x) • please •
> of course • That sounds interesting. • Have you … before? • That's great.

Mrs B	Tim will be back soon, Florian. How are you? Is everything OK?
Florian	Yes, _____
	_____
Mrs B	We're all fine too. I've just made some tea. Would you like a cup?
Florian	Yes,_____.
Mrs B	Sugar?
Florian	No, _____. We're going to Bath on a school trip tomorrow.
Mrs B	_____
	_____
Florian	Yes, but I haven't seen the Baths yet. We're going to do that tomorrow. Have you seen them?
Mrs B	Yes, _____. They're very interesting. But Tim liked the souvenir[2] shop a lot …

Did you know?
Roman people said 'Salve!' when they met a friend. It means 'Hello!' in Latin[1].

Roman Baths? No, thank you. That's not for me!

5 WORDS   Places in town   ▶ p. 97

Which is which? Match the descriptions and colour the places. Use the same colours.

You can buy lots of different food and drinks here.	department store
There are lots of beds in this building.	police station
You can buy stamps here. You can also get money.	supermarket
You can go here for help if somebody has stolen your bike.	post office
You can spend lots of time and lots of money in this building. They've got everything.	chemist
You can buy things here if you have a cold, a headache or a sore throat. You can also buy things like make-up or soap.	hospital

6805

¹ Latin ['lætɪn] *Latein*   ² souvenir [ˌsuːvəˈnɪə] *Andenken, Souvenir*

6 READING   Where are the shops?   ▶ p. 97

Lucy is telling Becky about some new shops. Read the dialogue carefully and write the names of the shops and the buildings on the street plan below.

Lucy	Have you seen the new shops in Elm Street? There's a big department store, a chemist, a pizza restaurant, ...
Becky	Hey, wait. Are there any clothes shops or shoe shops?
Lucy	I think there's a clothes shop next to the post office, and the shoe shop is next to the new chemist.
Becky	And where's the pizza restaurant?
Lucy	Hmmm, let me think. Oh, it's opposite the new internet café.
Becky	And where's that?
Lucy	The internet café is between the post office and the new department store.
Becky	And where's the new department store?
Lucy	Oh, it's opposite a cinema. The Odeon, I think. And you know where the police station is ...?
Becky	No, I don't know where the police station is.
Lucy	Oh. Well, if you're standing in Elm Street in front of the new chemist, the police station is on the right. And the new pizza restaurant is on the left, on the corner.
Becky	So the police station is behind the chemist and the shoe shop. Right?
Lucy	Yes, that's right, if you're standing in Mill Street opposite the post office.
Becky	Can you explain again, please, Lucy? That wasn't very clear.
Lucy	OK. Well, if you're standing in front of the cinema, the restaurant is on the right, the department store is opposite and the internet café is between the department store and the post office.
Becky	Oh. Hmmm. Well, that's better. Now I understand. Why didn't you say that before?

ELM STREET

post office

cinema

MILL STREET

supermarket

7 LISTENING   Where's Elm Street?   ▶ p. 97 🎧 15

Becky asks the way to Elm Street. Listen to the directions and draw the way on the map. Write the names of the streets and the buildings on the way there.

7007

Now you

Choose a place you often walk to: your school, your friend's home, the nearest supermarket, ... Explain how to get there from your home. You can use: **go along, turn right, turn left, go straight on, cross the road, on the right/left, on the corner of ..., opposite ...**

To get to my friend's home, you go to the right and cross the road at ... Street. Then you go along ...

8 What were the Muddles doing yesterday? (Past progressive) ▶ p. 98 • GF 22 (p. 146)

What were they doing at these times?

1

| 8.00 |
| make |

At 8 o'clock Mrs Muddles _was making breakfast._ _____

_____

2

| 8.30 |
| walk/to school |

At 8.30 Micky and Maggie _____

_____.

3

| 9.00 |
| drive/to work |

At 9 o'clock Mr Muddles _____

_____.

4

| 12.45 |
| eat |

At 12.45 Micky and Maggie _____

_____.

5

| 3.45 |
| go |

At 3.45 Max _____

_____.

7109

9 What was happening? (Past progressive) ▶ p. 98 • GF 22 (p. 146)

What was happening yesterday when Max looked through the pet shop window? Look carefully at the picture for two minutes. Then do the exercise on the next page.

7110

Write what was happening when Max Muddles looked through the pet shop window.
Use the words in the boxes.

try to get the fish

play with a snake

sing loudly

feed the dogs with dog biscuits

run round the shop

jump down from a cupboard

sit on a woman's head

fly round the shop

1   When Max looked through the window, a blue parrot *was singing loudly.* _____

2   ...a red parrot _____ .

3   ...two boys _____ .

4   ...a black cat _____ .

5   ...four budgies _____ .

6   ...a little girl _____ .

7   ...lots of mice _____ .

8   ...a black and white cat _____ .

Now you

What were you and your family or friends doing at 8 o'clock last night?
Write a short paragraph (at least five sentences).

At 8 o'clock last night I _____

_____

_____

_____

_____

_____

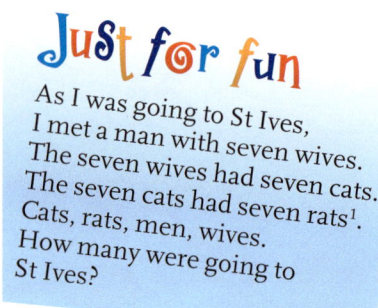

Just for fun

As I was going to St Ives,
I met a man with seven wives.
The seven wives had seven cats.
The seven cats had seven rats[1].
Cats, rats, men, wives.
How many were going to
St Ives?

[1] rat [ræt] *Ratte*

10 STUDY SKILLS   Correcting mistakes ▸ p. 99 • SF (p. 124)

Here is an e-mail from Sophie's e-friend in Germany. In your exercise book, write it again without the spelling mistakes (blue). Find three more spelling mistakes at the end of the text.

Deer Sophie,

How are you? Is school OK? We went on a trip yesterday to the Deutsches Museum in Munich[1]. We went by

bus and than on the underground. On the way their our teacher told us about the museum. There's so

much to sea, planes, cars, old things, and a fantastic modell railway. I realy enjoyed it.

At lunch time we ate our sanwiches in the museum café. I bought too postcards from the book shop. I

took some fotos of the most intresting things. There were lots of visiters. There was an english school

class too. When we left the wether was great. The sun was shineing, so the teacher bought us an

ice creme. Today we had to right a report about the trip. Have you been on a trip too? Tell me about it.

Love Angelika

7311

11 WRITING   My best/worst school trip ▸ p. 99

Write an e-mail to your e-friend about your best or worst school trip. For ideas look at Jo's report on p. 99 and exercise 12 on p. 104 of your student's book. Write at least five sentences.

12 REVISION   In the summer holidays (going-to future) ▸ p. 99 • GF 7 (p. 131)

*Write what you **are going to do** in the holidays. Ideas: **swim, play on the beach, do lots of sport, go on trips with your family, sleep late, go cycling with your friends**. Then write what you **aren't going to do**. Write two paragraphs in your exercise book (at least eight sentences).*

I'm *going to sleep* and eat, watch TV and relax... Or am I *going to stay* with Aunt Mildred again? Oh no!

7313

[1] Munich ['mjuːnɪk] *München*

13 QUIZ About Book 2 ▶ p. 99

a) How quickly can you do this quiz? Circle the right answer. You need the numbers in brackets ( ) in part b).

1 Who went to New York in the last summer holidays?

| Dan and Jo. (5) | Ananda. (12) | Ananda and Dilip. (8) |

2 Jody is ...

| Sophie's friend. (15) | the girl from St Ives. (1) | the new girl in 8PK. (7) |

3 Whose mum lost her job?

| Sophie's mum. (19) | Jack's mum. (16) | Ananda's mum. (22) |

4 Who has a good idea for a project on recycling clothes?

| Lesley. (16) | Ananda. (13) | Sophie. (5) |

5 What does Ananda find in the yard?

| Two baby frogs. (3) | Two baby hedgehogs. (25) | Two baby moles. (21) |

6 Why is Scruffy in the Dogs Home? Because ...

| Lesley doesn't want him. (6) | Lesley's dad can't have a pet. (8) | he ran away. (4) |

7 Dan and Jo go to visit their grandparents in ...

| Bath. (1) | Wales. (15) | Cornwall. (18) |

8 What does Emma make for the twins?

| A fruit salad. (20) | A chocolate cake. (24) | A pie. (12) |

9 The Thompsons don't go to the Brecon Beacons because ...

| Grandpa has no time. (19) | Jo wants to chat to his mum. (14) | Dan is ill. (9) |

10 Who is Bryn?

| A paramedic. (4) | A fireman. (5) | A caretaker. (11) |

11 The Llandoger Trow is ...

| a train station. (2) | a pirate pub. (1) | a Georgian house. (17) |

12 Who said: 'You really have to look after your things better, you know'?

| Mr Hanson. (23) | Miss White. (16) | Mr Smith. (25) |

13 In Bath a group of students visited the ... with Miss White.

| Theatre Royal (21) | Herschel Museum (19) | Museum of Costume (5) |

b) Now use the numbers in ( ) after your answers to read the code. If your answers are correct, the letters make a message.

1	2	3	4	5	6	7	8	9	10	11	12	13	14	15	16	17	18	19	20	21	22	23	24	25	26
A	B	C	D	E	F	G	H	I	J	K	L	M	N	O	P	Q	R	S	T	U	V	W	X	Y	Z

The message is: _H_   !

1 Which parts go together?

Write four new words.

centre   post   police   office

store   station   department   leisure

1 _____   3 _____

7501 2 _____   4 _____

2 Correct the mistakes.

There's one spelling mistake in each sentence.

1 The sun was shineing when we left home.   _____

2 On the bus everybody was chatting happyly.   _____

3 The bus stoped near the museum.   _____

7502 4 Suddenly Jo disapeared.   _____

3 Describe the pictures.

What were they doing yesterday at these times? Complete the sentences with the past progressives of cycle, sit, take *and* wait.

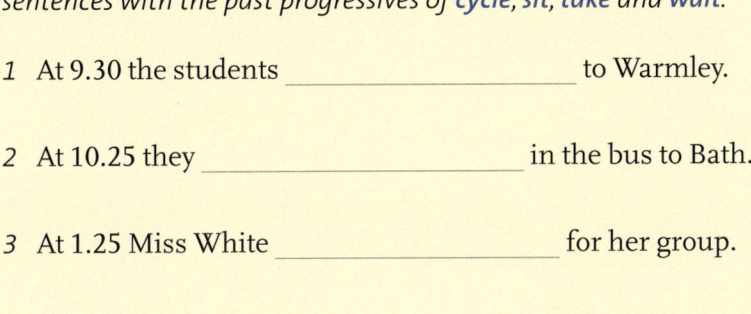

1 At 9.30 the students _____ to Warmley.

2 At 10.25 they _____ in the bus to Bath.

3 At 1.25 Miss White _____ for her group.

7503 4 At 3.30 Jo _____ photos.

4 Complete the words.

Ananda   Excuse me, please. Can you tell me the w_____ to the ice rink?

Woman   Oh, well, I've got a m_____ here, so I can show you where it is. Look. You

go s_____ on up this street, then you turn l_____ into George Street. Go

7504   p_____ the post office, then c_____ Albert Street and you'll see it on the corner.

18 points

● **Now you**

7505
7506
What do you think is good about school trips? What do you think is bad? Write two short paragraphs in your exercise book.
Ideas: interesting, better than lessons, have fun with friends and teachers, boring, maybe weather bad, ...

Jetzt kann ich ...

	Sehr gut!	OK	Verbessern!

HÖREN: Ich kann ...

... die Anweisungen, Fragen und Erklärungen meiner Lehrerin/ meines Lehrers verstehen. ☐ ☐ ☐

... mündliche Beiträge meiner Mitschüler/-innen verstehen. ☐ ☐ ☐

... die Listening-Aufgaben in meinem Buch/Workbook verstehen und bearbeiten. ☐ ☐ ☐

... die Vokabeln der Units 5 und 6 verstehen. ☐ ☐ ☐

... die Hörtexte der Units 5 und 6 ohne Mühe verstehen. ☐ ☐ ☐

SPRECHEN: Ich kann ...

... ein Brettspiel auf Englisch spielen, da ich dazu die notwendigen Vokabeln und Redewendungen beherrsche (z.B. *dice*; *It's your turn. Move back two spaces.*). ☐ ☐ ☐

... bei einer Diskussion in kurzen Sätzen meine Meinung zu einem Thema oder einer Geschichte sagen, auch wenn ich kleine Fehler mache. ☐ ☐ ☐

... die Wörter der Units 5 und 6 korrekt aussprechen und anwenden. ☐ ☐ ☐

... nach dem Weg fragen und jemandem den Weg erklären. ☐ ☐ ☐

... mich freundlich auf Englisch unterhalten (z.B. mit *Yes, thank you. I'm fine, thanks. How are you? What about you? See you later.*). ☐ ☐ ☐

LESEN: Ich kann ...

... die längeren Erzähltexte der Units 5 und 6 lesen und verstehen. ☐ ☐ ☐

... die längeren Erzähltexte der Units 5 und 6 ohne Mühe laut lesen. ☐ ☐ ☐

... längere Sachtexte lesen und verstehen. ☐ ☐ ☐

... Texte verstehen, indem ich versuche, unbekannte Wörter zu erschließen. ☐ ☐ ☐

SCHREIBEN: Ich kann ...

... einen kurzen Bericht über eine Klassenfahrt/einen -ausflug schreiben. ☐ ☐ ☐

... einen kurzen Sachtext zu einem bekannten Thema schreiben. ☐ ☐ ☐

... meine Texte sinnvoll gliedern. ☐ ☐ ☐

... die Wörter der Units 5 und 6 richtig schreiben. ☐ ☐ ☐

LAND UND LEUTE: Ich habe ...

... einiges über die Geschichte, über berühmte Menschen (z.B. Brunel, Cabot) und über die Sehenswürdigkeiten Bristols gelernt. ☐ ☐ ☐

... etwas über die Geschichte und Sehenswürdigkeiten Baths gelernt, z.B. über den Einfluss der Römer in und um Bath. ☐ ☐ ☐

Jetzt kann ich ...   Sehr gut! | OK | Verbessern!

GRAMMATIKVERSTÄNDNIS: Ich kann ...

... mit *am/are/is* + *going to* + Infinitiv über Absichten und Pläne für
die Zukunft sprechen (z.B. *I'm going to start my project tomorrow*). ____ ☐ ☐ ☐

... mit *who, which* und *whose* Relativsätze bilden (z.B. *The student
who likes football is Jo*). ____ ☐ ☐ ☐

... die Verlaufsform der Vergangenheit *(past progressive)* richtig erkennen
und bilden (z.B. *I was reading/they were writing*). ____ ☐ ☐ ☐

... mit dem *past progressive* ausdrücken, dass etwas zu einem bestimmten
Zeitpunkt in der Vergangenheit im Gange war (z.B. *Yesterday at 4 o'clock
I was reading a book*). ____ ☐ ☐ ☐

VOKABELVERSTÄNDNIS: Ich kann ...

... einige Wörter für Gebäude und Orte in der Stadt richtig verwenden
(z.B. *post office, police station, hospital, market, ice rink*). ____ ☐ ☐ ☐

... Wörter und Redewendungen, die ich für eine Wegbeschreibung brauche,
richtig verwenden (z.B. *Can you tell me the way to ...?; turn right/left,
go straight on*). ____ ☐ ☐ ☐

SKILLS – LERNEN UND ARBEITEN: Ich ...

... kann eine Multiple-Choice-Aufgabe bearbeiten. ____ ☐ ☐ ☐

... kann einen Text markieren, um bestimmte Informationen
zu kennzeichnen. ____ ☐ ☐ ☐

... kann meine Texte in Einleitung, Mittelteil und Schluss gliedern. ____ ☐ ☐ ☐

... weiß, wie ich am besten meine Texte auf Fehler und Verständlichkeit
überprüfen kann. ____ ☐ ☐ ☐

WAS ICH FÜR MEIN ENGLISCHLERNEN GETAN HABE: Ich habe ...   häufig | manchmal | nie

... den Unterrichtsstoff zu Hause noch einmal aufmerksam
wiederholt. ____ ☐ ☐ ☐

... mir viel Mühe mit meinen Hausaufgaben gegeben. ____ ☐ ☐ ☐

... die vorgeschlagenen Aufgaben im Grammar File bearbeitet. ____ ☐ ☐ ☐

... die vorgeschlagenen Aufgaben in meinem Skills File bearbeitet. ____ ☐ ☐ ☐

WIE ICH MICH VERBESSERN KÖNNTE: Ich könnte ...

... mit den Listenings und den Pronunciation –
Übungen in meinem Buch/Workbook meine
Aussprache gezielt verbessern. ____ ☐

... Sätze und Ausdrücke, die in bestimmten
Situationen nützlich sind, auswendig lernen. ____ ☐

... immer daran denken, meine Texte sinnvoll
zu gliedern, d.h. in Einleitung, Mittelteil
und Schluss. ____ ☐

... immer daran denken, meine Absätze
mit einem *topic sentence* zu beginnen. ____ ☐

... so oft wie möglich versuchen, meine
Englischkenntnisse aktiv einzusetzen,
z.B. im Urlaub. ____ ☐

▸ Hier kannst du deine Antworten im Checkpoint überprüfen. Falls du Probleme mit den jeweiligen Aufgaben hattest, folge den Lernhilfen in der rechten Spalte. Die Verweise beziehen sich auf dein Schülerbuch oder dein Workbook.

▸ Deine Punktzahl kannst du ermitteln, indem du dir für jede richtige Lösung einen Punkt gibst. Schreib deine Gesamtpunktzahl in das gelbe Kästchen unten links.

1 What's the weather like?

1 It's *rainy*   .

2 It's *cloudy.*

3 It's *foggy.*

4 It's *windy.*

4 P.

▸ Schau dir im Skills File in deinem Buch den Punkt *Learning words - Step 1* (S. 115) noch einmal an.

▸ Lern die Wörter mithilfe des Vocabulary (S. 150–152).

2 That's wrong!

1 *Lesley didn't try to be nice.*

2 *She didn't want to come to Bristol.*

3 *Jack didn't fly to New York.*

4 *Jo didn't run to get help for Jody.*

4 P.

▸ Lies dir das Grammar File 2 (S. 128) zur Verneinung des *simple past* durch.

▸ Löse die Aufgabe 9a im Practice-Teil deines Buchs (S. 19).

3 Ask Ananda questions.

1 *Where did you go?*

2 *How long did you stay?*

3 *What was the weather like?*

4 *What did you do?*

4 P.

▸ Wie du Fragen im *simple past* bildest, kannst du im Grammar File 3 (S. 128) nachlesen.

▸ Bilde Fragen zur Übung 12a im Practice-Teil (S. 20).

4 Describe the picture.

1 Ali is *on the right*   .

2 Sue is *on the left*   .

3 Pat is *between Sue and Ali*   .

4 Ed is *behind Pat*   .

4 P.

▸ Schau dir im Skills File den Abschnitt zu *Describing pictures* an (S. 117).

▸ Nimm dir ein Foto und beschreibe es.

● **Now you** (Musterlösung)

On the first day of school after the holidays we got a new form teacher. First he/she gave us our new timetable, but he/she didn't give us any homework. Then I saw my old friends and we talked about the holidays. We got some new books for English, German and Maths, but we didn't do much work.

▸ Falls du Schwierigkeiten hattest, einen zusammenhängenden Text zu schreiben, schau dir im Skills File den Abschnitt zu *Linking words and phrases* (S. 123) an.

▸ Wiederhole die Übung 6 im Practice-Teil (S. 18).

▸ Schreib deinen Text zur Aufgabe 9 im Workbook (S. 8) noch einmal in dein Heft.

▸ Lern die Formen des *simple past* (Grammar Files 1–2, S. 127–128).

Ich habe _____ Punkte von 16.

16–14   Sehr gut. Weiter so!
13–11   Schon recht gut.
Unter 11 Genauer lernen!

Falls du Probleme hattest:

1 Clothes: write the names.

1	*skirt*	4	*trousers*
2	*shirt*	5	*(baseball) cap*
3	*blouse*	6	*jacket*

6 P.

▸ Schau dir im Skills File den Abschnitt zu *Learning words - Step 1* (S. 115) noch einmal an.
▸ Lern die Wörter mithilfe des Vocabulary (S. 156–157).
▸ Löse die Aufgabe 2a/c im Practice-Teil (S. 33).

2 Find group words for these things.

1 *sports gear*

2 *free-time activities*

3 *head*

4 *clothes*

4 P.

▸ Schau dir im Skills File den Punkt *Learning words - Step 2* (S. 115) noch einmal an.
▸ Wiederhole die Übung 1 im Practice-Teil (S. 33).

3 Complete with *mine*, *yours*, ...

Tim	Is this old jacket ___*yours*___, Becky?
Becky	No, it isn't ___*mine*___ . Ask Mum. Maybe it's ___*hers*___ . Or ask Dad.
Tim	Ask Dad? It isn't ___*his*___ . It's pink with little white rabbits!

4 P.

▸ Lies dir das Grammar File 5 (S. 130) zu Possessivpronomen durch.
▸ Löse die Aufgabe 3a im Practice-Teil (S. 34).

4 Compare with *than*.

1 Art – Music: easy
   I think ... is easier than ...

2 detective stories – animal stories: exciting
   I think ... are more exciting than ...

3 Sophie – Emily: nice
   I think ... is nicer than ...

4 the Simpsons – Mr Bean: funny
   I think ... is/are funnier than ...

5 a summer holiday – a holiday in the snow: good
   I think ... is better than ...

6 a boring Sunday – a long school day: bad
   I think ... is worse than ...

6 P.

▸ Im Grammar File 8 (S. 132–133) findest du Informationen zur Steigerung der Adjektive.
▸ Wiederhole die Übungen 11a (S. 36) und 15 (S. 38) im Practice-Teil.

● **Now you** (Musterlösung)

I spend my pocket money on comics or magazines. I don't buy clothes or stuff for school. Sometimes I buy sweets and drinks or ice cream after school. I spend most money on magazines and cinema tickets. I don't get much pocket money, so I don't save much.

▸ Schau dir im Skills File den Abschnitt zu *Mind maps* (S. 116) an. Dort erfährst du, wie du deine Ideen sammeln und ordnen kannst.
▸ Die Schülerbuchseiten 26–27 können dir inhaltliche Informationen liefern.

Ich habe [   ] Punkte von 20.

20–17	Sehr gut. Weiter so!
16–13	Schon recht gut.
Unter 13	Genauer lernen!

Falls du Probleme hattest:

1 What is it?

1 *a squirrel*
2 *a monkey*
3 *a hippo*
4 *a bear*
5 *a deer*
6 *a lion*

6 P.

> ▸ Schau dir im Skills File die Punkte *Learning words - Step 1* und *Step 2* (S. 115) noch einmal an.
> ▸ Lern die Wörter mithilfe des Vocabulary (S. 161, 163).
> ▸ Wiederhole die Übung 1a im Practice-Teil (S. 50).

2 What will the weather be like?

1 In England it ___*'ll*___ be sunny and it ___*won't*___ rain.
2 In Scotland it ___*'ll*___ rain, but it ___*won't*___ be cold.

4 P.

> ▸ Die Formen und den Gebrauch des *will-future* findest du im Grammar File 9 (S. 134).
> ▸ Löse die Aufgaben 2a (S. 50) und 3a (S. 51) im Practice-Teil.

3 What will happen if …?

1 If I ___*find*___ (find) a hedgehog baby, I ___*'ll have to*___ (have to) give it water.
2 It ___*'ll get ill*___ (get ill) if I ___*give*___ (give) it milk.
3 If I ___*don't keep*___ (not keep) it warm, it ___*won't survive*___ (not survive).

6 P.

> ▸ Die Bedingungssätze (Typ 1) werden im Grammar File 10 (S. 135) erklärt.
> ▸ Üben kannst du sie, indem du die Aufgabe 5 im Practice-Teil (S. 52) wiederholst.

4 Describe the pictures.

1 Dan is running ___*fast*___.
2 Sophie is riding her bike ___*carefully*___.
3 Ananda is working ___*hard*___.
4 Mr Kingsley is shouting ___*angrily*___.

4 P.

> ▸ Wie du die Adverbien der Art und Weise bildest und verwendest, erfährst du im Grammar File 11 (S. 136–137).
> ▸ Löse die Aufgabe 11a im Practice-Teil (S. 54).

● **Now you** (Musterlösung)

When I'm 25, I think I'll still live in Germany. I'll have an interesting job, but maybe I won't live in the same town. I think I'll have a little car, but I won't have a big house or a plane. I'll probably have a small flat. Maybe I'll speak very good English, but I won't work in England.

> ▸ Schau dir die Formen und den Gebrauch des *will-future* im Grammar File 9 (S. 134) noch einmal an.
> ▸ Der Punkt *Mind maps* im Skills File (S. 116) gibt dir Informationen, wie du deine Ideen sammeln und ordnen kannst.

Ich habe _____ Punkte von 20.

20–17	Sehr gut. Weiter so!
16–13	Schon recht gut.
Unter 13	Genauer lernen!

Falls du Probleme hattest:

1 What's in the picture?

1 river
2 sheep
3 factory
4 castle
5 railway
6 P. 6 field

▸ Schau dir im Skills File die Punkte *Learning words - Step 1* und *Step 2* (S. 115) noch einmal an.
▸ Lern die Wörter mithilfe des Vocabulary (S. 165–166).
▸ Wiederhole die Übung 1b im Practice-Teil (S. 66).

2 Write correct sentences.

1 I'll be at the station at five-thirty.
2 P. 2 We were in the DVD shop till six.

▸ Über die Wortstellung informiert dich das Grammar File 12 (S. 138).
▸ Löse die Aufgaben 2 und 3a im Practice-Teil (S. 66), um sicherer Sätze bilden zu können.

3 What have they done?

1 Ananda ___has found two hedgehogs___ .
2 Jo ___has dropped some glasses___ .
3 The Thompsons ___have packed a picnic___ .
4 P. 4 Emma ___has made a pie___ .

▸ Schau dir die Grammar Files 13–15 (S. 139–141) an, um den Gebrauch und die Formen des *present perfect* besser zu beherrschen.
▸ Um sicherer im Gebrauch zu werden, mach die Übungen 6–8 im Practice-Teil (S. 68–69).

4 Complete the words.

Mum   Tim, what's the m ___atter___ ?
      Are you feeling i ___ll___ ?
Tim   Yes, my throat h ___urts___ and I have
      a t ___emperature___ . And my head.
      I have a h ___eadache___ too. And my
      legs hurt when I m ___ove___ . I can't
      go to school today.
6 P. Mum   Really? But the French test is today...

▸ Lies dir in deinem Schülerbuch die S. 64 noch einmal durch. Dort findest du Redewendungen, die man benutzt, wenn man krank ist.
▸ Lern diese Wörter mithilfe des Vocabulary (S. 167–168).

● **Now you** (Musterlösung)

Germany is a big country. About 83 million people live here. Lots of people visit Germany too. Berlin is the biggest city. About 3.5 million people live there. There are many interesting places to visit and lots of things to do. You can visit museums, churches and old buildings.
Germany is a beautiful country too. It has got nice cities and lakes, sea and beaches too. The biggest mountain is the Zugspitze. It's 2,962 metres. You can go up the mountain on a railway, or you can walk!

▸ Falls du Schwierigkeiten hattest, einen zusammenhängenden Text zu schreiben, schau dir im Skills File den Punkt zu *Mind maps* (S. 116) und *Topic sentence* (S. 123) an.
▸ Die Übung 4 im Practice-Teil (S. 67) kann dir dabei helfen, deinen Text besser zu strukturieren.

Ich habe		Punkte von 18.

18–16	Sehr gut. Weiter so!
15–13	Schon recht gut.
Unter 13	Genauer lernen!

1 What's the opposite?

1 open — *closed*

2 rich — *poor*

3 arrive — *leave*

4 friendly — *unfriendly*

5 possible — *impossible*

6 P. 6 agree — *disagree*

2 Complete the sentences.

1 Cabot was the explorer
who found Newfoundland.

2 Who is the famous engineer
whose statue stands in Bristol?

3 Nick Park is the man
who invented Wallace and Gromit.

4 P. 4 The Bristol Balloon Fiesta is an event
which takes place in a park in August.

3 Complete the words.

Assistant   Hi. What can I g *et* you?

Tim   I'd like a s *moothie* , please.

Assistant   What f *lavour* would you
like? Today we've got banana,
strawberry, orange and kiwi too.
6 P. They're all d *elicious* and
very h *ealthy* .

4 Circle the correct question tag.

Tim   This is a cool juice bar, (isn't it?) / is it?

Lucy   Yes, and the people are friendly,   isn't it? /
(aren't they?)

Tim   And it wasn't too expensive,   wasn't it? /
(was it?)

Lucy   And the smoothies were great,
4 P. (weren't they?) / were they?

● **Now you** (Musterlösung)

*I like teamwork. It's nice to talk about ideas and do
work with classmates. I have done teamwork for
German. It's interesting to do teamwork for
projects. Everybody in the team can find out
different information from the internet. You can
do a presentation in teamwork too.*

Ich habe ⬚ Punkte von 20.

20–17	Sehr gut. Weiter so!
16–13	Schon recht gut.
Unter 13	Genauer lernen!

Falls du Probleme hattest:

▸ Schau dir im Skills File die Abschnitte zu
Learning words - Step 1 und *Step 2* (S. 115) noch
einmal an.
▸ Du findest diese Gegensatzpaare im Vocabulary
häufig mit diesen schwarzen Pfeilen ◂ ▸
(S. 154, 170–173).

▸ Wie du Relativsätze richtig bildest und
verwendest, erfährst du im Grammar File 17
(S. 142).
▸ Löse die Aufgaben 5a (S. 83) und 8 (S. 84) im
Practice-Teil.

▸ Lies dir die S. 80 in deinem Buch noch einmal
durch. Dort erfährst du, wie man sich ein
Getränk bestellen kann.
▸ Lern die Wörter mithilfe des Vocabulary
(S. 170–172).

▸ Im Grammar File 18 (S. 143) erfährst du, wie
man *question tags* richtig bildet und verwendet.
▸ Übe den Gebrauch der *question tags* mithilfe der
Aufgabe 10 im Practice-Teil (S. 86).

▸ Schau dir im Skills File den Abschnitt zu
Mind maps (S. 116) an, um deine Gedanken
besser ordnen zu können.
▸ Denk an ein Projekt/eine Arbeit in der Schule,
das/die du im Teamwork gemacht hast.

Falls du Probleme hattest:

1 Which parts go together?

1 *leisure centre*

2 *post office*

3 *department store*

4 P. 4 *police station*

▶ Schau dir im Skills File die Abschnitte zu *Learning words - Step 1* und *Step 2* (S. 115) noch einmal an.
▶ Lern diese Wörter mithilfe des Vocabulary (S. 175–176).
▶ Löse die Aufgabe 1a im Practice-Teil (S. 100).

2 Correct the mistakes.

1 *shining*

2 *happily*

3 *stopped*

4 P. 4 *disappeared*

▶ Lies im Skills File die Seite zu *Correcting mistakes* (S. 124).
▶ Wiederhole die Übung 12a im Practice-Teil (S. 104).

3 Describe the pictures.

1 At 9.30 the students _*were cycling*_ to Warmley.

2 At 10.25 they _*were sitting*_ in the bus to Bath.

3 At 1.25 Miss White _*was waiting*_ for her group.

4 P. 4 At 3.30 Jo _*was taking*_ photos.

▶ Im Grammar File 22 (S. 146) erfährst du, wie du das *past progressive* formst und wann du es verwendest.
▶ Üben kannst du das *past progressive* mithilfe der Aufgaben 8a und 9 im Practice-Teil (S. 102–103).

4 Complete the words.

Ananda   Excuse me, please. Can you tell me the w *ay* to the ice rink?

Woman   Oh, well, I've got a m *ap* here, so I can show you where it is. Look. You go s *traight* on up this street, then you turn l *eft* into George Street. Go p *ast* the post office, then c *ross* Albert Street and you'll see it on the corner.

6 P.

▶ Schau dir die S. 97 in deinem Buch noch einmal an. Dort findest du die Redewendungen, die du brauchst, um nach dem Weg zu fragen oder einen Weg zu beschreiben.
▶ Such dir in deiner Umgebung eine Straße/ein Gebäude aus und beschreibe von deiner Wohnung/deinem Haus aus den Weg dorthin.

● **Now you** (Musterlösung)

School trips are interesting. You can go to a museum or visit an old town and see something new. You can have fun with friends and teachers. It's better than lessons.
School trips can be boring too. Maybe it's cold and rainy, but you have to go. You have to stay together with the class and with the teachers.

▶ Mit einer Mindmap (Skills File, S. 116) solltest du zuerst deine Gedanken zu Klassenfahrten/ -ausflügen sammeln und ordnen.
▶ Auf der S. 123 im Skills File findest du Hilfestellungen, wie du deinen Text geschickt mit *linking words* verbindest, deinen Text in Absätze einteilst und deine Absätze einleitest.

Ich habe _____ Punkte von 18.

18–16	Sehr gut. Weiter so!
15–11	Schon recht gut.
Unter 11	Genauer lernen!

Unit 1

GF 1 REVISION The simple past: positive statements ▸ *GF (p. 127)*

We **were** in Spain **last summer**. It **was** great.
We **went** swimming a lot and **played** volleyball on the beach.
Wir waren letzten Sommer in Spanien/sind letzten Sommer in Spanien gewesen ...

Mit dem *simple past* kannst du über Vergangenes berichten, z.B. wenn du eine Geschichte erzählst.
Das *simple past* steht häufig mit Zeitangaben wie *last summer*, *yesterday*, *three weeks ago*, *in 2004*.

a) (to) be and regular verbs

Our holiday **was** fantastic. We **were** in New York. We **stayed** for two weeks. And Jay **played** basketball every day!

Beim *simple past* von *be* gibt es nur zwei Formen:

I, he/she/it **was** *you, we, they* **were**

Bei **regelmäßigen Verben** wird *ed* an den Infinitiv angehängt:
stay → *stayed*, *play* → *played*

Es gibt für **alle** Personen nur eine Form.

b) Irregular verbs

The Carter-Browns **went** to Majorca.
(Infinitiv: **go**)
Dan and Jo **met** a nice girl in Cornwall.
(Infinitiv: **meet**)

Wie im Deutschen gibt es auch im Englischen eine Reihe von unregelmäßigen Verben, deren *simple past*-Formen du einzeln lernen musst.

▸ *Unregelmäßige Verben (pp. 220–221)*

GF 2 REVISION The simple past: negative statements ▸ *GF (p. 128)*

Sophie: Lesley **didn't want** to come to Bristol.
Ananda: She **didn't say** much.
But we **didn't ask** her much.

Eine Aussage im *simple past* verneinst du immer mit
didn't + **Infinitiv** (Langform: *did not*).
❗ (Nicht: *Lesley didn't wanted* ...)

Merke:		
Simple present	I **don't get up** early.	Lesley **doesn't get up** early.
Simple past	I **didn't get up** early.	Lesley **didn't get up** early.

GF 3 REVISION The simple past: questions and short answers ▸ *GF (p. 128)*

Did Jo **help** Jody? – Yes, he **did**. / No, he **didn't**.
Did the girls **talk** to Lesley? – Yes, they **did**. / No, they **didn't**.
Why did Jody **need** help?

Fragen im *simple past* bildest du mit **did**:
Did Jo help?
❗ (Nicht: *Did Jo helped?*)
Das Fragewort steht wie immer am Anfang.

Merke:		
Simple present	Do you **get up** early?	Does Lesley **get up** early?
Simple past	Did you **get up** early?	Did Lesley **get up** early?

GF 4 Subject and object questions with *who* and *what* ▸ *GF (p. 129)*

Who liked the new girl, Sophie? And **what happened** on holiday?

Wer mochte das neue Mädchen, Sophie? Und was geschah in den Ferien?

Who did you **see** in school, Sophie? And **what did** you **do**?

Wen hast Du in der Schule gesehen, Sophie? Und was habt ihr gemacht?

◂ **Subjektfragen** („Wer oder was?"-Fragen) bildest du ohne *do/does/did*. Die Wortstellung bei Subjektfragen ist wie in Aussagesätzen. Das Fragewort ist das Subjekt des Fragesatzes:

	S	V	O
Fragesatz:	**Who**	liked	the new girl? (**Wer** ...?)
Aussagesatz:	*Nobody*	liked	the new girl.

◂ **Objektfragen** („Wen/Wem oder was?"-Fragen) bildest du im *simple present* mit *do/does* und im *simple past* mit *did*. Das Fragewort ist das Objekt des Fragesatzes:

O		S	
Who	did	you	see? (**Wen** ...?)
What	did	you	do?

Unit 2

GF 5 **Possessive pronouns** ▸ *GF (p. 130)*

my dog	mine	*meiner, meine, meins*	**our** room	ours	*unserer, unsere, unseres*
your dog	yours	*deiner, deine, deins*	**your** room	yours	*eurer, eure, eures*
his dog	his	*seiner, seine, seins*	**their** room	theirs	*ihrer, ihre, ihrs*
her dog	hers	*ihrer, ihre, ihrs*			

GF 7 **The *going to*-future** ▸ *GF (p. 131)*

Ananda: **I'm going to help** Dad in the shop next Sunday.

Ich werde nächsten Sonntag Vater im Laden helfen. / Ich habe vor, ... zu helfen.

Ananda: Jay, **are** you **going to visit** us next year? **When are** you **going to come**?

Jay, wirst/willst du uns nächstes Jahr besuchen? Wann wirst du kommen?

Wenn du über **Absichten** und **Pläne** für die Zukunft sprechen willst, verwendest du das Futur mit *going to*.
Es wird mit *am/are/is going to* + **Infinitiv** gebildet.
Die Kurzformen heißen *I'm/you're/he's going to* usw.
◂ Fragen kannst du **mit Fragewort** (*When ...?*) oder **ohne Fragewort** (*Are you ...?*) stellen.

Positive statements		Negative statements		Questions and short answers
I'm going to		I'm not going to		Are you going to watch TV?
You're going to		You aren't going to		– Yes, I am. / No, I'm not.
He's/She's going to		He/She isn't going to		
We're going to	read.	We aren't going to	play.	Is Jo going to watch TV?
You're going to		You aren't going to		– Yes, he is. / No, he isn't.
They're going to		They aren't going to		

GF 8 **The comparison of adjectives** ▸ *GF (pp. 132–133)*

a) Comparison with *-er/-est*

How old are the Carter-Brown children?
– Well, Sophie is young. She's twelve now. Toby is younger. He's nine. Baby Hannah is the youngest, and Emily is the oldest.

Steigerungsformen verwendest du, um Personen oder Dinge miteinander zu vergleichen, z.B.:

young [jʌŋ]	jung
younger ['jʌŋgə]	jünger
(the) youngest ['jʌŋgɪst]	der/die/das jüngste ...; am jüngsten
old	alt
older	älter
(the) oldest	der/die/das älteste ...; am ältesten

Die Steigerung mit *-er/-est* verwendest du für
– einsilbige Adjektive (*young, full, nice, big, ...*) und
– zweisilbige Adjektive mit der Endung *-y* (*pretty, funny, easy, ...*).

b) Comparison with *more/most*

I think tennis is **boring**. But basketball is even **more boring**. And yoga is the **most boring** thing of all.

Andere Adjektive werden mit *more* und *most* gesteigert:

boring	langweilig
more boring	langweiliger
(the) most boring	der/die/das langweiligste ...; am langweiligsten

c) Irregular comparison

Ananda has got a good idea, but Sophie's idea is better. Lesley has got the best idea.

Jo hasn't got much money this week. Dan has got more, but Dilip has got the most.

Einige Adjektive werden unregelmäßig gesteigert:

good	–	*better*	–	*best*
bad	–	*worse* [wɜːs]	–	*worst* [wɜːst]
much/many	–	*more*	–	*most*

Die Steigerung der Adjektive

Mit *-er/-est*:	Mit *more/most*:	Unregelmäßig:
Einsilbige Adjektive:	Andere zwei- und mehrsilbige Adjektive:	
old – older – oldest	boring – more boring – most boring	good – better – best
Adjektive auf *-y*:	terrible – more terrible – most terrible	bad – worse – worst
happy – happier – happiest	exciting – more exciting – most exciting	much/many – more – most

d) *bigger than* – *as big as*

Sophie, Hip is so big. I think your rabbit is **bigger than** my cat.

But your cat is **faster than** Hip.

Is your cat as **fast** as my rabbit?
Ist deine Katze so schnell wie mein Kaninchen?
I think she's faster. But she is**n't** as **big** as your rabbit.

◄ Wenn Personen oder Dinge **unterschiedlich** groß/schnell/alt/… sind, vergleichst du sie mit der 1. Steigerungsform + *than* („als"):

Your rabbit is   bigger   than   *my cat.*   (… größer als …)
Your cat is   faster   than   *Hip.*   (… schneller als …)
▲
1. Steigerungsform

! (Nicht: … *bigger/faster ~~as~~* …)

◄ Wenn Personen oder Dinge **gleich** groß/schnell/alt/… sind, vergleichst du sie mit *as big/fast/old/… as*.
(Verneint: *not as big/fast/old/… as*)

Unit 3

GF 9 The *will*-future ► *GF (p. 134)*

The hedgehogs **will be** cold tonight. I'**ll have to** take them inside.

Maybe their mother **will come**. But maybe she **won't**.

Ananda: **What** will **they** need? Do you know?
Will **they** want milk?
Sophie: **No, they** won't.

Um auszudrücken, was in der Zukunft geschehen wird, benutzt du *will* + **Infinitiv**. Es gibt für **alle** Personen nur eine Form. Die Kurzform von *will* ist *'ll: I'll, you'll* usw.

Das *will-future* steht häufig mit Zeitangaben wie *tomorrow, next month, soon, in a few weeks*.

Die **verneinte Form** von *will* heißt **won't**. (Langform: *will not*).

Fragen kannst du mit **Fragewort** (*What will they …?*) oder **ohne Fragewort** (*Will they …?*) stellen.
Die Kurzantworten lauten: *Yes, I will / No, I won't* usw.

GF 10 Conditional sentences (type 1) ► *GF (p. 135)*

Sophie: If you **give** a hedgehog water, it'**ll be** happy.
Wenn du einem Igel Wasser gibst, wird er zufrieden sein.
Sophie: If you **don't keep** it warm, it **won't survive**.
Wenn du ihn nicht warm hältst, wird er nicht überleben.

if-Satz (Bedingung) ▼	Hauptsatz (Folge für die Zukunft) ▼
*If you **give** a hedgehog water,*	*it'**ll be** happy.*
*If you **don't keep** it warm,*	*it **won't survive**.*
Im *if*-Satz steht das *simple present*.	Im Hauptsatz steht meist das *will-future*.

GF 11 Adverbs of manner ► *GF (pp. 136–137)*

a) Use

Hedgehogs are **slow** and **quiet**.

Hedgehogs walk slowly and quietly.

◄ Ein **Adjektiv** beschreibt ein **Nomen** näher.

◄ Ein **Adverb der Art und Weise** beschreibt ein **Verb** näher.

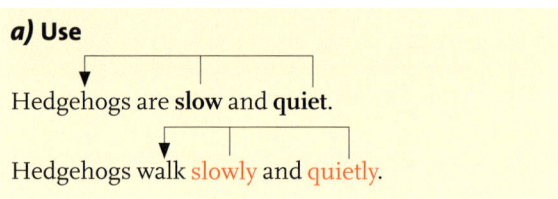

b) Regular forms

Adjektiv	slow	→	slowly	**Adverb**
	quiet	→	quietly	
	careful	→	carefully	

Die meisten Adverbien der Art und Weise entstehen durch Anhängen von **-ly** an das Adjektiv.

c) Irregular forms

She did a **good** job with the babies.   (Adjektiv)
She did the job well.   (Adverb)

Jo: The rabbits are very **fast**.   (Adjektiv)
Dan: Of course! All rabbits can run fast. (Adverb)

Ananda: It's **hard** work at the clinic.   (Adjektiv)
Steve: The volunteers work very hard. (Adverb)

Einige Adverbien haben eine unregelmäßige Form, die du auswendig lernen musst:

– Das Adverb zu *good* heißt *well*.

– Bei *fast* und *hard* sind Adjektiv und Adverb gleich.

d) Word order

'You killed the hedgehogs,' she shouted angrily.

Steve fed **the babies** carefully.

Steve fütterte vorsichtig die Babys.

Das Adverb der Art und Weise steht direkt **nach dem Verb**.

! In Sätzen mit Objekt steht es **nach dem Objekt**.

Unit 4

GF 12 Word order   ▸ GF (p. 138)

a) REVISION   S – V – O

Jack writes stories.

Die Wortstellung im Aussagesatz lautet
S – V – O (**S**ubjekt – **V**erb – **O**bjekt).

What do you do **when you** come home?
Was machst du, **wenn du nach Hause** kommst?

Anders als im Deutschen ist auch im Nebensatz die Wortstellung **S – V – O**.
Denk dabei an die <u>S</u>traßen-<u>V</u>erkehrs-<u>O</u>rdnung.

b) Place before time

Grandpa: We can go **to the mountains in the morning**.
Wir können morgen Vormittag in die Berge fahren.

Wenn Ortsangaben (*to the mountains*) und Zeitangaben (*in the morning*) zusammen am Satzende stehen, dann gilt: **Ort vor Zeit**.

Ort	Zeit
... to the mountains	in the morning.

GF 13 The present perfect: use   ▸ GF (p. 139)

Grandma: Hurry up, boys! I've **cooked** your breakfast and Grandpa **has packed** a picnic.

Mit dem *present perfect* drückst du aus, dass jemand etwas getan hat oder dass etwas geschehen ist. Dabei ist **nicht wichtig, wann** es geschehen ist. Deshalb wird auch kein genauer Zeitpunkt genannt.

GF 14 The present perfect: form   ▸ GF (pp. 139–140)

a) The past participle

Das *present perfect* wird mit *have/has* und der 3. Form des Verbs gebildet. Die 3. Form des Verbs heißt **Partizip Perfekt** (*past participle*).

1 Grandpa **has** packed a picnic.

1 Bei regelmäßigen Verben hängst du *ed* an den Infinitiv an:
  *pack + ed → pack*ed.

2 The twins **haven't** seen Caerphilly Castle.
  Dan doesn't feel well, so he **hasn't** eaten his breakfast.

2 Unregelmäßige Verben haben eigene Formen, die du einzeln lernen musst. Unregelmäßige Verben werden immer so angegeben: *(to) see, saw, **seen**   (to) eat, ate, **eaten**.*
  Die 2. Form ist die *simple past*-Form *(saw, ate),*
  Die 3. Form ist das *past participle (seen, eaten).*

  ▸ *Unregelmäßige Verben (pp. 220–221)*

b) Positive and negative statements

Positive statements		Negative statements		Long forms
I've packed		I haven't seen		I/You/We/They have (not) packed
You've packed		You haven't seen		He/She has (not) packed
He's packed		He hasn't seen		
She's packed	a picnic.	She hasn't seen	Dan.	I/You/We/They have (not) seen
We've packed		We haven't seen		He/She has (not) seen
You've packed		You haven't seen		
They've packed		They haven't seen		

c) Questions and short answers

Have the twins been to the Brecon Beacons?
– Yes, they have. / No, they haven't.

Bei Fragen im *present perfect* werden Subjekt und *have/has* vertauscht. Kurzantworten werden mit *have/has* gebildet.

GF 15 The present perfect with adverbs of indefinite time ▸ *GF (p. 141)*

Grandpa: I've already packed the car.
Ich habe schon das Auto beladen.

Grandma: Oh, good. Have the twins had breakfast yet?
Haben die Zwillinge schon gefrühstückt?

Grandpa: I've just seen Jo in the kitchen.
But Dan hasn't come down yet.

Das *present perfect* drückt aus, dass etwas <u>irgendwann</u> geschehen ist. Daher findest du oft **Adverbien der <u>unbestimmten</u> Zeit** in *present perfect*-Sätzen:

already	schon, bereits;	*just*	gerade (eben), soeben
not ... yet	noch nicht;	*yet?*	schon?
ever?	jemals? / schon mal?		

Unit 5

GF 17 Relative clauses ▸ *GF (p. 142)*

who, which, that

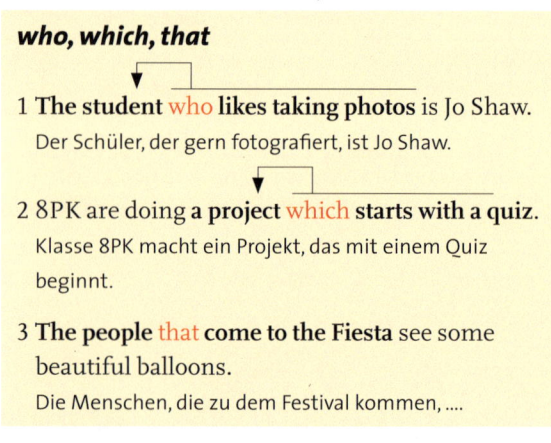

1 **The student** who **likes taking photos** is Jo Shaw.
Der Schüler, der gern fotografiert, ist Jo Shaw.

2 8PK are doing **a project** which **starts with a quiz.**
Klasse 8PK macht ein Projekt, das mit einem Quiz beginnt.

3 **The people** that **come to the Fiesta** see some beautiful balloons.
Die Menschen, die zu dem Festival kommen, ...

◀ 1 Das Relativpronomen *who* steht in Relativsätzen, die **Personen** beschreiben: *The **student/woman/people** who ...*

◀ 2 Das Relativpronomen *which* steht in Relativsätzen, die **Dinge (und Tiere)** beschreiben: *The **project/things/animals** which ...*

◀ 3 Das Relativpronomen *that* kannst du für Personen und Dinge verwenden.

GF 18 Question tags ▸ *GF (p. 143)*

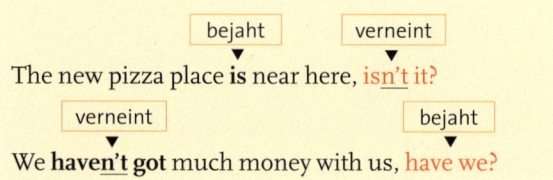

The new pizza place **is** near here, isn't it?

We **haven't got** much money with us, have we?

◀ Wenn der Aussagesatz bejaht ist, ist das Frageanhängsel verneint.

◀ Wenn der Aussagesatz verneint ist, ist das Frageanhängsel bejaht.

Unit 6

GF 22 The past progressive ▸ *GF (p. 146)*

Yesterday at one o'clock Form 8PK and their teachers were having lunch.
Gestern um ein Uhr aßen die Klasse 8PK und ihre Lehrer gerade zu Mittag.

Jack was telling jokes, but Jo wasn't listening.
Jack erzählte Witze, aber Jo hörte nicht zu.

Das *past progressive* drückt aus, dass etwas zu einem bestimmten Zeitpunkt in der Vergangenheit gerade im Gange war. Die Handlung oder der Vorgang war noch nicht abgeschlossen.

Das *past progressive* wird mit *was/were* + *-ing*-Form gebildet. Die verneinten Formen heißen *I wasn't listening/ you weren't listening/he wasn't listening* usw.